Stop Bedwetting in Seven Days

A simple step-by-step guide to help children conquer bedwetting problems

ALICIA EATON

First published by MX Publishing, 2009

Second edition published by Matador Publishing, 2011

This edition published by Practical Inspiration Publishing, 2019

© Alicia Eaton, 2019

The moral rights of the author have been asserted.

ISBN 978-1-78860-111-5 (print)
   978-1-78860-109-2 (mobi)
   978-1-78860-110-8 (epub)

Illustrations by Imogen McGuinness

Cover photography by Brian Hubbard -
Studio 86 Photography

 Practical Inspiration
PUBLISHING

Also By Alicia Eaton

Words That Work: How to Get Kids to Do Almost Anything

Wouldn't it be wonderful if you could simply wave a magic wand and have your kids do as they were asked, first time around? Imagine a life where you could put an end to all those arguments about homework, bedtimes, screen time and mobile phones – not to mention mealtime nightmares with fussy eating and junk food cravings.

And, if you've ever felt 'lost for words' dealing with a child's feelings of anxiety or lack of confidence, *Words That Work* also offers solutions to common parenting problems such as a fear of dogs, spiders, doctors and dentists.

Discover how changing the words you use can bring about a change in a child's behaviour.

'A great read – I highly recommend you grab your copy now.'
Sue Atkins, ITV's *This Morning* parenting expert and author of *Raising Happy Children for Dummies*

'A very informative and useful book – Alicia will help you consider what you say.'
Felix Economakis, BBC psychologist on *Panic Room* and *Freaky Eaters*

Strategies with rewarding outcomes.'
Lorrine Marer, Channel 5 behavioural specialist on *The Teen Tamer and Families Behaving Badly*

Fix Your Life with NLP: A First-Aid Kit for the Mind

It's often said our minds are like computers, so it's not surprising that we sometimes download unwanted habits, behaviours and patterns of thinking, much like a computer virus. How much easier would life be if we could simply install anti-virus software for our minds?

Fix Your Life will show you how you can do just that. In this book, Alicia Eaton cuts through the technical jargon usually associated with NLP and explains how techniques and strategies regularly used by some of the most successful people in the world can easily be incorporated into your daily life – bringing about amazing changes.

Whether you're struggling with a lack of confidence, anxiety, panic attacks, insomnia, binge eating or an addiction to Facebook, this book will show you how easy it really can be to re-programme your mind and 'fix' it.

'Entertaining, practical and meticulously researched… first aid for whatever life throws at you.'
Dr Stephen Simpson, mind coach and best-selling author of *Get Lucky Now*

Please see the website shop at www.aliciaeaton.co.uk for full details of these books and Alicia's MP3 audio recordings.

Praise for this Book

'*Stop Bedwetting in Seven Days* is a very good book. I have found it to be clear, effective and have recommended it to a number of my patients.'

Dr Anne Wright, consultant paediatrician, Evelina Children's Hospital, Guy's and St Thomas' NHS Trust

'This is a must-have for parents struggling to handle bedwetting. This great book is bursting with practical advice and simple ideas that really work.'

Sue Atkins, ITV's *This Morning* parenting expert and author of *Raising Happy Children for Dummies*

'I have used this book with a number of patients and thoroughly recommend it. A very effective method of treating this embarrassing problem.'

Dr Jo Waddell, GP and NLP trainer

'This book brings together the best of modern thinking about neurological development and I have no hesitation recommending it to parents and clinicians as an approach to explore before more invasive remedies are considered.'

Dr Mark Chambers, GP and integrated health care practitioner

Contents

Introduction

Welcome to the 10th anniversary edition of *Stop Bedwetting in Seven Days*. When first released back in 2009, many were sceptical that a programme using the latest psychological techniques such as visualisation exercises and hypnotherapy could help solve a problem like children's bedwetting.

Fortunately, much has changed over the last 10 years and we live in more enlightened times. Our knowledge of neuroscience, brain plasticity and how our thoughts change our physiology is better understood and my programme no longer sounds so 'alternative'.

I started seeing children for bedwetting problems in my Harley Street practice in 2004 and became increasingly worried at the growing number (many of them teenagers) who, through no fault of their own, were stuck with this miserable habit. Bedwetting not only creates an embarrassing pile of wet laundry but also dents a child's confidence and their social development, with sleepovers and school trips causing stress and anxiety. Sometimes the problem can even change the course of a young person's life. I've worked with more than one child who had to decline a part in a well-known London theatre production because the role demanded they live in the theatre company's children's house for a period of six weeks – and bedwetters simply weren't allowed.

Worse still, I was unhappy at seeing so many children on prescription medications that dry up bodily fluids, in the hope that these would solve the problem. Often they don't and I've seen many children with side effects such as very dry skin and constant headaches that impair schoolwork. If these drugs don't work, then an antidepressant may be prescribed, in the hope that it will have a relaxing effect on the bladder and stop it from emptying at night.

Somewhere along the line, I felt we'd lost our way in tackling this problem. My instincts are that bedwetting is not a problem that children should have to put up with, until they 'grow out of it', as so many of the experts would have us believe – nor should they have to take drugs. The solution lies *inside* the body rather than *outside* in the form of alarms and medications.

There's a complex coordination that needs to take place between the mind and body. New neural pathways need to be made in the brain in order to control the bladder more efficiently and achieve night-time dryness.

Some 10 years ago, I pointed out that it was no coincidence that as night-time pull-up pants became ever more absorbent, with the aim of keeping a child's skin even drier, the more we were seeing children with incontinence issues. It's not unusual nowadays for some of them to start primary school still wearing nappies. Our skin is an important human organ sending vital messages up to the brain – when we interfere with this communication, problems will naturally occur. I'm pleased to see many more health professionals are now taking my advice on board and recommending night-time protective pants be stopped after the age of 5.

My behavioural change programme incorporates visualisation techniques and success strategies from the fields of positive psychology, hypnotherapy, mindfulness and neuro-linguistic programming (NLP). People are often surprised when I tell them that I help children overcome their problems using these types of therapies.

A young child's brain is in its most fertile developmental phase with new neural pathways being created all the time – this is the perfect time to be using techniques that support their development, rather than waiting until they acquire a problem and trying to fix it later.

Top athletes regularly use these types of techniques to enhance their performance. A recent study in the *Journal of Neurophysiology*[1] found that simply

---

[1] B.C. Clark, 'The power of the mind: the cortex as a critical determinant of muscle strength/weakness' in *Journal of Neurophysiology*, 112 (12), 3219–3226 (2014).

imagining exercise can tone muscles and even make them stronger, which is why top athletes regularly use visualisation techniques to enhance their performance.

It makes perfect sense to solve a problem like bedwetting through the power of the mind, rather than prescribing expensive medications that no parent wants to use and that cost the health service unnecessary expenditure. It also makes perfect sense for all of us to use these methods to tackle ordinary everyday problems, rather than simply applauding Wimbledon finalists and Olympic runners when they use them.

Sales of this book now run into the thousands and children from all parts of the world have successfully fixed their bedwetting habits by using it. Each day I receive emails from grateful parents not only in the UK, but also the United States, Canada, Australia, New Zealand, Hong Kong, South America, all parts of Europe and Scandinavia.

I'm now regularly asked to train other practitioners in my methods and hypnotherapists as far away as India are adopting my system for use with their own clients.

My own survey, in which 165 parents took part, showed that over 70% of children achieved dry nights following this system and 85% of parents would recommend this system to others.

Using the feedback that I've received over the years from both parents and children, I've updated the *Stop Bedwetting in Seven Days* method to make it better than ever before. And, I'm delighted to be able to say that so many more people – parents, GPs, consultant paediatricians – are now acknowledging the value of using a behavioural approach to solve this widespread problem.

1

•

Bedwetting
What's it all about?

If you have a child that wets the bed, you might be feeling as if you are the only parent in the world whose child has this unwanted habit. It can be difficult to discuss the subject with family and friends, leaving you at a loss to understand why your child has failed to stop a habit that so many other children seem to get over with ease.

If this sounds familiar, then take comfort from knowing that more than 750,000 children in the UK accidentally wet their beds at night. Bedwetting still occurs on most nights in 15% of all 5-year-olds and is still a problem for 3% of all 15-year-olds. The numbers are just an estimate, of course, because bedwetting is not a subject that parents are happy to discuss openly. In many cases, it isn't even a subject that is talked about within the family.

The truth is that millions of children all over the world wet their beds or have to rely on protective pants every single night. If your child is one of them, it is very likely that there are at least one or two more in their class at school with the same problem.

You are not on your own and the good news is that bedwetting can be overcome.

For a number of years, I have been helping parents and their children to conquer this habit. I have seen the consequences of bedwetting – children suffer from a lack of confidence and low self-esteem, often failing to reach their full potential. Invitations to sleepovers with other children have to be refused, school trips and camps are met with fear and family holidays are not the relaxing times they are meant to be.

Let me put your mind at ease by reassuring you that bedwetting can be cured and the positive effects on your child will be amazing. Solving your child's bedwetting problem is much more than just achieving night-time dryness – it is about giving your child an increase in their level of self-confidence both at home and at school, which can lead to improved performance in the classroom and better interaction with their peers.

My reason for writing this book is that I believe the process I have successfully developed over a number of years can be easily learned by parents.

In order to solve problems, we often need to *stop* things happening. And the best way to do this is to *think* carefully about what you do want to happen and then *plan* how to be successful.

With this book, I've done the work for you and devised a plan that will enable you and your child to achieve that success. The effects on your child once they've got rid of the bedwetting habit will be life-changing. The effects on you, as a parent, will be equally liberating and rejuvenating!

Before we look at how my programme could help you and your child, let's have a look in more detail at what this problem is all about.

Bedwetting – also known as nocturnal enuresis – affects most children up to the age of 3 as the development of bladder function control can be a slow process. Bedwetting can continue to be quite common in children up the age of 8 and sometimes even into their teenage years.

Studies show that bedwetting children who are given professional help and advice are more likely to become dry than those who aren't.[2] With one or two children in every 100 failing to achieve night-time dryness, it is vitally important to get help at the right time. Some children never quite 'grow out' of their bedwetting habit, often carrying the scars into adulthood. Prolonged childhood bedwetting can manifest itself in many ways, such as difficulties forming relationships and getting jobs, susceptibility to stress, anxiety and even depression.

HOW COMMON IS BEDWETTING?

Bedwetting is a common problem, especially in children under the age of 5. According to figures published by the *British Medical Journal*, at the age of 5 as many as 20

---

[2] M.T. Grzeda, J. Heron, K. Tilling, A. Wright and C. Joinson, 'Examining the effectiveness of parental strategies to overcome bedwetting: an observational cohort study', in *BMJ: Paediatrics Research*, 7 (7) e016749 (2017).

children in 100 will have difficulty in controlling their bladders at night-time.[3]

By age 7, this figure has dropped to around 8 children in every 100, so we can see that most children will develop that vital mind/body link at around the age of 6 years.

It's at this age that children enter a new developmental phase. A good indicator of this happening is the loss of milk teeth. If your child still wets the bed at night and is starting to lose teeth, I'd recommend introducing this system – it shows it's the right time and will support their natural development.

The research goes on to show that by age 10, there are still 5 children in every 100 experiencing problems. So, not much progress is made with children who are left waiting for nature to take its course.

You may hear many reasons being put forward as possible causes of a bedwetting problem, such as:

- the size of the bladder
- a urinary tract infection
- lack of hormones to concentrate urine
- something that runs in families
- stress or anxiety

---

[3]   BMJ figures as cited in P.H. Caldwell, D. Edgar and J.C. Craig, 'Bedwetting and toileting problems in children', in *Medical Journal of Australia*, 182 (4), 190–195 (2005).

Because of the stigma attached to bedwetting, most people start their search for help through the Internet. Type 'bedwetting' into your computer and you will be given a number of different treatment options ranging from the use of electronic alarms, medication to concentrate the flow of urine or even antidepressants.

If your child is failing to get dry at night after the age of 5, your first port of call should be a visit to the doctor's surgery. It's best to rule out more serious underlying causes such as infections and even diabetes. All being well (and in the overwhelming majority of cases, it is), you'll probably be advised to wait for your child to 'grow out of it'.

I know so many parents find this frustrating. It's so open-ended, giving no clues as to how long you might have to wait, and they rarely give advice about how to tackle the problem in the meantime.

Statistics in the *British Medical Journal*[4] show around 15% of bedwetting children get dry at night each year – they are the ones who 'grow out of it'. So that leaves 85% who don't and to my mind, that's just too many. Why sit and wait, when there is something you can do about it?

---

[4]   W.I. Forsythe and A. Redmond, 'Enuresis and spontaneous cure rate', in *BMJ: Archives of Disease in Childhood*, 49, 259–263 (1974).

It is true that most children do eventually grow out of the bedwetting habit, but around 1% of 18-year-olds remain stuck in this cycle of behaviour and can continue to wet the bed throughout their adult life. Helping your child to break this habit of behaviour at age 6, 7 or 8 is a lot easier than when they're ready to fly the nest and head off to university! By that age, their self-confidence will have taken a knock as they will have experienced problems with sleepover parties and school trips.

BEDWETTING ALARMS

If your child doesn't spontaneously grow out of their bedwetting habit, you'll be advised to try an alarm. These clip on to the child's pants or directly on to the bed sheet and buzz, vibrate or ring when wetness is detected. Alarms have differing levels of success and many parents tell me their child sleeps right through the noise the alarm makes and wakes up everyone else in the house instead, including siblings. I am not against the use of alarms, but it's best to be aware that initially the alarm is for the parent, whose job is to quickly go to the child on hearing the alarm, get them up out of bed and guide them to the toilet. It can take quite a while (three months) for your child to respond to the alarm themselves and be quick enough to stop wetting the bed completely.

If alarms are not successful, children may be prescribed medication or drugs to concentrate their urine and, in extreme cases, they will be offered antidepressants.

Our bodies release a hormone while we sleep and this helps to concentrate our urine. When children struggle to control their bladders at night, it's often assumed that an absence of the hormone is the cause of this. Doctors, however, do tell me that there is no definitive test to check whether this is the case in each particular child and so the use of a drug called Desmopressin – a synthetic hormone that mimics the action of the real hormone – is really a 'best guess'.

It should solve the problem pretty much immediately, if it's going to work at all, but I have come across children who have been taking it for many months, and some even for years, without achieving dry nights – it can still be a hit-and-miss affair. After this time, it's very likely that it's not going to work at all and if your child is in this situation, I would recommend a return visit to the practitioner who prescribed it for you, with a view to stopping it altogether.

Some children will be told they have 'twitchy' or irritable bladders and if your child is one of these, they will probably also have trouble during the daytime with frequent visits to the toilet and urge incontinence too. The antidepressant imipramine is commonly prescribed to help relax the muscles of the bladder. To be honest, I found it quite shocking when I first discovered this, as there are better ways of relaxing different parts of the body – namely, through the power of the mind.

It's also important to note that if your child is using medication on rare occasions only, such as sleepover parties and school trips, then they should be aware of the need to restrict fluids in the evening. Your child has to be responsible enough to police themselves and refuse drinks (perhaps tricky to do if they are at a party) or you will have to inform the host so they can keep an eye on them. Otherwise the medication may cause side effects and it's best to be aware of these.

I know that each of these methods have differing levels of success and many parents do say that the alarms or medication have worked for their child. I am always pleased to hear this, for I know the stress, anxiety and problems with social development that this miserable habit creates for children – so a win is a win.

However, in my experience of helping children with a bedwetting condition, these methods often only manage the problem in the short term rather than cure it for good and around 70% of children will go back to their old habits and behaviours after two to three months. I helped one couple who had tried three different alarms, each of which had terrified their child, before consulting their family doctor who prescribed medication to reduce the flow of urine, only it never did. This process went on for nearly two years before they brought their child to see me. Two years – that's a lot of wet sheets and pyjamas!

I believe a better solution to this problem is one that starts 'from within' rather than from some sort of external crutch.

Just like a smoker who quits cigarettes with the aid of nicotine replacement gum, or an overweight person who loses weight by drinking diet shakes instead of eating proper food, the problem may appear to have been solved, but quickly returns once the crutch is taken away.

Only changes made on the 'inside' can be guaranteed to produce long-lasting results on the 'outside'.

I'd also like to encourage parents to try my behavioural change method *before* going down the road of seeking medical intervention.

Not only will it save our NHS a vast amount of money, but doctors and nurse practitioners are hugely in favour of my programme because it educates and informs parents so they can take appropriate steps to help their child.

This system will help your child develop self-awareness and recognise that it is indeed possible to fix one's own problems and be successful. This is such an important *life skill* and so many children who have followed my programme have gone on to use the same methods to help them with their exams or sporting achievements.

There's a complex coordination that needs to take place between the nerves and the muscles of the bladder and, more often than not, a delay in this happening is what holds children back.

New neural pathways or connections need to be made in the brain in order to achieve night-time dryness and I'm going to show you how easy it can be to speed this process up.

TEENAGERS

If you're reading this and have a teenager who still wets the bed at night, please don't despair. Over the years, I have worked with many teenagers in my Harley Street practice – most of which have been referred to me by hospital consultants. Having undergone all the treatment and investigations available, be it scans, medications, alarms, etc., they're sent to me as a last resort.

I don't think it's a coincidence that most of these teenagers fix their problem after one or two sessions with me.

So what is it that I do differently? I know that I'm not a genius, I'm not special and I don't have a magic wand, but it helps to have a positive mindset when tackling this problem and certain techniques that help to put the past in the past. When you can step out from the shadow of your disappointments, exciting changes can begin to take place.

IS IT CAUSED BY EMOTIONAL PROBLEMS?

For many years, it was assumed that bedwetting was triggered by anxiety or emotional problems and this encouraged many parents to keep even more quiet about the problem. Fortunately, we live in more enlightened times now and there's a greater awareness about the fact that we all suffer ups and downs in our emotional well-being, so discussing these matters is so much easier.

In the 15 years that I've been seeing children with bedwetting, I have found the overwhelming majority of children to be happy, well-adjusted, performing well at school and have great friends. Their only problem is being stuck with a bedwetting habit that they never grew out of. It's a habit, nothing more, and it's referred to as 'primary enuresis'.

Of course, there are downsides to being a bedwetting child and it does cause embarrassment and anxiety for most of them, but this occurs as a result of the problem and not the other way around.

In fewer cases, there can be a sudden onset of bedwetting. If your child has been dry at night for several months or even years and starts wetting the bed again, this can be caused by an emotional upset such as a change at home, family illness or stress with schoolwork. This is usually temporary and not the same as an ongoing bedwetting problem and is referred to as 'secondary enuresis' – the bedwetting is not the primary source of the problem. The best way to solve the wetting problem is to offer support and help for the primary problem.

As a parent, you will probably be able to tell the difference between a behaviour that's habit-based and one that's triggered by something else. Go with your instincts but monitor the situation carefully and ask for a second opinion if you're not sure.

CHILDREN WITH SPECIAL NEEDS

I'm often asked if my programme is suitable for children with conditions such as Down's syndrome, autism, dyslexia or dyspraxia. I'm pleased to say that I have been contacted by many parents of children with special needs, whose children have achieved success after being told by other health professionals that it simply would never happen. However, as I know you'll already know, every child is unique so it's not possible to predict an exact outcome, but there's certainly no need to assume that your child can't be helped. You can read detailed testimonials from the parent of an older child with Down's syndrome and another who was born with hypospadias, on my website.

2

•

Understanding Habits and Behaviours

GETTING INTO THE HABIT

In the overwhelming majority of bedwetting cases, the cause is simply *habit*. Somehow over the years, your child got into a habit of wearing pull-up pants or similar absorbent protection and just never learnt how to stay dry all night. It's as simple as that.

And then you found yourselves caught in that 'catch-22' situation: never quite confident enough to stop using absorbent pants (after all, think about the embarrassment an accident would cause if your child is staying away from home) – but at the same time never quite giving your child's mind the opportunity to allow the neurological pathways to wire themselves up and create that 'autopilot'.

It's a common enough problem and in fact, it's the reason why more and more children are beginning to suffer from night-time bedwetting problems than ever before. Have you noticed how the supermarket shelves are increasingly stocking night-time 'pull-up' protective pants for teenagers up to the age of 15?

Twenty or so years ago these just did not exist to the same extent. Make no mistake, the manufacturers are more than happy to keep on making these in all sorts of fancy designs and colours to keep your child happy. But I believe these may well be the cause of the problem, rather than the solution. As the range of products available to help bedwetting children broadens – dry-night pants, bed mats, protective covers for duvets, waterproof inner liners for sleeping bags – the more this normalises the problem and keeps us stuck in our ways. I often wonder whether communities living in the wilds of Africa have as many children as we do suffering from irritable, small bladders that can't cope with hanging on to urine all night long. Somehow I suspect they're more in tune with their bodies.

PAST GENERATIONS

Quite a few of the bedwetting problems parents encounter today are a result of lifestyle changes that have taken place in our society and the changes in our toilet-training methods in general.

It's not uncommon nowadays to hear grandparents proudly announce that they never had problems toilet-training their young babies. And according to some – like my own mother – it was all over and done with by the age of 12 months! Of course, today's mums will roll their eyes up to the ceiling and take this piece of information with a pinch of salt.

But back in the days before disposable nappies had been invented, the incentive to get your baby dry and out of nappies was very much greater. Changing terry cloth nappies was hard work with hours of cleaning, boiling, sterilising and washing on a daily basis. Being a 'stay-at-home' mum was not so much a lifestyle choice but more of a necessity – someone had to do it.

And 'staying at home' also meant staying in one place for most of the day – making it very much easier to build up a routine for toilet-training. Modern-day mums are much more likely to be working outside the home, resulting in young children being ferried to and from nurseries or childminders.

Even our shopping habits have changed – most of us can spend several hours on a large supermarket visit rather than a quick 20-minute daily trip to the local shops, as was often the case years ago. Nowadays, it's a brave mother who's willing to chance her luck doing the shopping with a toddler in the throes of toilet-training. All this moving around, usually by car, makes dealing with 'accidents' that much harder.

Today's children have busy social lives and many start having sleepovers with friends at a much earlier age than they used to. So, it's only natural that we do everything we possibly can to avoid those embarrassing accidents and encourage our children to continue wearing nappies or pull-ups for much longer.

The nappy manufacturers have done everything they can think of to make our lives easier and over the years they've improved the quality, fit and design to such an extent that your child no longer has to even feel wet when they urinate. How comfortable can life get?

It's no wonder toilet-training can become a bit of an uphill struggle for many parents – let's face it, life has to get a lot worse before it gets any better. Is there ever a good time to take off those nappies?

Eventually, pretty much all children will become toilet-trained during the day – it just happens a little later nowadays than it used to. Getting dry at night then becomes the next hurdle and if it doesn't happen spontaneously, this is where many parents get stuck, not knowing quite how to move their child on to the next stage and make this happen.

THE TRUE VALUE OF AN ACCIDENT

Avoiding accidents can mean missing out on valuable learning opportunities. Babies growing up before the days of disposable nappies very quickly made a connection between urinating and feeling wet. Once this link was established, a second one was made – a relaxing of the bladder muscles and the release of urine.

And once you learn how to start something, you can quickly learn how to stop it. Constant repetition of a piece of behaviour – literally, your child weeing over and over again throughout the day – is what allows that vital mind–body connection to become more established. Having these experiences enables your child's mind to begin to understand how to change their behaviour.

Knowing this, it becomes easier to see why so many more children nowadays are struggling to master the art of bladder control. Not only are they missing out on the valuable learning opportunities that numerous toilet accidents throughout the day would have given them, but they're also missing out on the experience of feeling wet as the quality of nappies or pull-ups improves.

The human brain can be likened to a piece of plastic that moulds and adapts to fit the experiences in our environment. If your child never experiences the feeling of wetness when releasing urine from the bladder, those valuable connections in the brain cannot be made.

Each time any of us undertakes a brand new activity such as riding a bicycle, tying a shoelace, learning to drive a car or dance the tango, a new neural pathway is created in our brain. Each time we repeat this new activity or pattern of behaviour, imagine a crackle of electricity travelling down this pathway over and over again. With time, the more we repeat the activity, the more the neural pathway becomes established. This new behaviour then becomes part of what we call our 'subconscious' mind.

By doing something over and over again, you will start to change the structure of the brain – the new pattern of behaviour becomes 'hard-wired' and an automatic habit. And this is what my programme is designed to achieve for your child.

THE POWER OF BELIEF

Whether you believe you can, or believe
you can't – you're probably right.

(Henry Ford)

Your child's self-image plays a crucial role in predicting whether or not your child will overcome this problem successfully. Once the idea of being a bedwetter has established itself in your child's mind, it can become a lot harder to change the pattern of behaviour, for our behaviours will always match our beliefs about our capabilities – i.e. the image we have of ourselves.

Our beliefs are a very powerful force and influence everything we do. Put simply, if you cannot 'see' yourself being successful then your chances of succeeding are much harder.

One of my favourite stories that demonstrates the power of our beliefs is the story of Roger Bannister, the first person to run a mile in under four minutes, back in 1954. For many years, runners had dreamed of breaking the record but none had been successful. Doctors had declared it an impossibility, fearing the heart would spontaneously combust under the pressure.

Bannister, however, was determined and against advice he organised a race that saw him not only achieve his goal of four minutes, but beat it with seconds to spare. News of his achievement spread around the world. So far so good.

But what is even more interesting is that while no one in the history of running had been able to achieve that record-breaking time, as soon as Bannister did it, other athletes went on to do exactly the same over the course of the next two years.

It would not have been surprising if one or two more runners had achieved the same time, but the fact that a whole cluster went on to also break that magical barrier confirms the theory that as soon as we start believing that something is possible, it becomes a lot easier for us to do it. The athletes had the concrete proof and evidence of Bannister's achievement to show them that running a mile in less than four minutes was truly possible. Their performances quickly changed to match their altered beliefs.

In just the same way, your child's self-image plays a crucial role in predicting whether or not your child will be successful. Once the idea of being a bedwetter has established itself in your child's mind, it becomes a lot harder to change the pattern of behaviour.

Our behaviours will always match the image we have of ourselves and my programme is designed to help your child develop the positive self-image that will make success that much easier to achieve.

I've devised this easy-to-read guide with activities and strategies for you and your child to follow over the course of seven days or so. It's designed to get that crucial brain activity working in the right way to get those new neural pathways established. We're going to speed up the body's natural processes.

For most children, sooner or later, those vital connections will end up being made – but why wait until your child is yet another year older? How many more sleepovers and school trips will be missed? How many more embarrassing moments will there be? And how much more washing will you tolerate? With this system, you'll be able to help your child beat this habit once and for all.

It is possible to get through all the exercises in this programme in less than seven days – some children who come to see me for a face-to-face appointment can be dry on the first night after just the initial session. However, it's not easy to predict how quickly your child's mind and body will start to create this new way of behaving.

Should you feel your child could do with some extra time to fully understand all the techniques, then it is possible to extend this programme for up to 14 days. However, do make sure your child gets daily practice, for the repetition, repetition, repetition will change the structure of the brain and is the key to success.

Do be aware though, that while it's going to take a week to work through all the brain-training exercises I've created, it can take a while longer for the new habit and behaviour to become established. Every child is unique so it is hard to predict how long it will take your child to become fully confident with staying dry at night, but rest assured progress is being made from the minute they start the programme. And if your child needs a little longer to get to grips with things, then that's ok too.

3

•

Creating Change with Hypnotherapy and NLP

WHAT'S THE ALTERNATIVE?

I believe the key to ending bedwetting once and for all is to encourage your child's mind and body to work more closely together. Children's minds are continually creating new connections to accommodate new patterns of thinking and behaviour.

I've been seeing children with bedwetting problems regularly since 2004 and in my practice I use a variety of techniques including hypnotherapy and neuro-linguistic programming (NLP). I believe I have developed a quicker, safer and more natural alternative for changing the night-time habits of bedwetting children for good, while also boosting their confidence and feelings of well-being.

Over the years, I noticed that the majority of children who came to see me for a face-to-face session were dry that same night. Keeping dry, however, often proved much harder, which is why I started giving visualisation exercises as homework and an audio recording to listen to as backup. The repetition of visualisation work produced far better results and was the reason for my packaging it up as this book. It isn't always instant success and there may be several wet nights in the first couple of weeks, but over a period of three to four weeks, a pattern of dry nights usually begins to get established.

HYPNOTHERAPY AND NLP – IT'S CHILD'S PLAY

While consulting a hypnotherapist may not be the solution that is uppermost in your mind to begin with, it is now becoming more widely accepted throughout the medical profession and many parents are referred to me by their family clinic and GP.

If the idea of hypnotising and reprogramming children's minds sounds a bit strange – fear not. During this stage of life, children's minds are like sponges, absorbing all sorts of information naturally. In other words, they are being 'hypnotised' all the time. You only have to observe a child's ability to gaze at the TV and recite the adverts back perfectly to see this in action.

That 'deeply relaxed state' is what we try to recreate during a session because, as you will have already witnessed when your child watches TV, information can be absorbed more deeply. In this instance, the information will be all about having dry beds forever.

Despite its complicated name NLP is really quite simple. It helps us to deal with what we think, what we say and what we do by breaking down our thought patterns and changing them for the better. Our thinking has a direct impact on our feelings and our behaviour.

Remember, your child's mind is being moulded and shaped by their environment all the time. In fact, your child spends many moments in a trance-like state every day, randomly absorbing all the messages around them.

Some of these messages are good ones, such as being praised for producing a good piece of homework, and others are not so helpful, such as having accidents and wetting the bed. Children quickly build up a picture of things they do well and things they do less well – and then go on to behave accordingly.

Techniques such as hypnotherapy and NLP are, in my opinion, under-utilised in the treatment of children, but more parents are now turning to them as traditional methods fail to help their children.

As a result of the general lack of understanding about how these methods work, we are still more likely to prescribe unnecessary drugs and medication for our children, such as general anaesthetics to overcome dental phobias and drugs to reduce the flow of urine, rather than consider safer, more natural alternatives.

CREATING AN AUTOPILOT

Conscious thinking uses different parts of the brain to unconscious learning so it's best to allow time for your child's brain to activate a deeper, more permanent intelligence.

After all, you're going to be asking your child to do things when they're half-asleep – in other words, not very conscious at all! The more deeply we can embed new patterns of behaviour on their subconscious minds, the easier it will be for them to operate on 'autopilot'.

Have you ever driven a car on a long journey and got to your destination unable to remember much about the driving part of it? That's because your conscious mind switched off for a while and started thinking about other things. Fortunately, the ability to drive has been imprinted on your subconscious mind – remember all those driving lessons you took? Your subconscious mind was able to take over and do the job for you – your very own automatic pilot.

And you're going to be able to do exactly the same for your child – creating an automatic pilot that can register signals from the bladder, wake them up and steer them in the direction of the bathroom in the middle of the night. It's easier than you think.

RESULTS OF MY SURVEY

After the first edition of this book had been available for six months, I carried out a survey by sending out emails asking a variety of questions. A total of 165 people replied and what follows is a summary of the results:

The age range varied from 4 years old to 14 years, so I have broken some of the results down by age group.

Overall, an overwhelming 85% of respondents said they would recommend this system to other parents. The results went on to show that 73% of children did achieve dry nights using the system.

For 58% of children this was three or more dry nights each week, compared to only 13% who were achieving this before carrying out the seven-day programme.

And for 30%, this was total dryness after following the seven-day programme, compared to zero at the start.

I looked more closely at the group of children who had *never* had any dry nights before in their lives and the results following the programme were as follows:

Age	Percentage achieving dry nights (%)
4	75.0
5	90.0
6	64.5
7	62.5
8	28.7
9	42.8
10	41.8
11	20.0
12	37.5
13	20.0
14	100*

* Just one respondent.

Not surprisingly, the figures for the younger age group were higher – leaving me to feel that just like learning how to swim, speak a foreign language or play a musical instrument, it's best to follow this type of programme as early as possible to avoid the wrong habits becoming deeply ingrained.

However, when I asked how many children who had already experienced *some* dry nights (but simply not enough) could see a marked improvement following the programme, the figures were much higher in the older age groups.

Age	Percentage achieving dry nights (%)
4	50
5	50
6	61
7	79
8	66
9	86
10	83
11	90
12	88
13	60
14	50

These results reflect the outcome after following the seven-day programme with reinforcement from listening to the audio programme and repetition of the visualisation exercises. Over the following months, these children can expect their results to continue improving until they reach 100% dryness.

There are a number of factors that can affect these results. As well as the age and psychological make-up of each child, there is also medical history and the parent's own relationship with the child, plus their personal interpretation of the programme, to be taken into consideration.

As parents, we all know how much easier it is for an 'outsider' such as a teacher or tutor to sit and work with our children, than it is for us. And I also appreciate that not every parent will be able to deliver the NLP techniques in the way that I can, following all my years of training.

However, following these positive results, I would very much hope that GPs, health visitors and enuresis clinics consider adopting these methods, training their staff and using them as a first resort, rather than recommending them as a last resort, which is often what happens. Not only will our children be healthier and happier, but both parents and hospitals will also save an enormous amount of money.

THE NORWEGIAN STUDY

In 2004, a study appeared in the *Journal of the Norwegian Medical Association* about using hypnotherapy to treat patients with chronic nocturnal enuresis.[5] This study consisted of 12 boys ranging in age from 8 to 16.

All the boys had been diagnosed with primary nocturnal enuresis and four were also diagnosed with diurnal enuresis (daytime accidental urination). All 12 participants reported an average of zero dry nights per week. The 12 participants also had a family history of bedwetting and had tried other forms of treatment such as bedwetting alarms and medication.

The boys had between two and eight hypnotherapy sessions as part of the study and also practised self-hypnosis for one month after the sessions.

Two follow-ups were performed at intervals of three months and one year. During both follow-ups, 9 out of the 12 participants reported seven out of seven dry nights per week. The researchers referred the three patients who continued to experience bedwetting to seek additional medical treatment.

---

[5] T.H. Diseth and I.H. Vandvik, 'Hypnotherapy in the treatment of refractory nocturnal enuresis', in *Journal of the Norwegian Medical Association*, 124 (4), 488–491 (2004).

The researchers concluded that hypnotherapy is an effective treatment for children diagnosed with nocturnal enuresis.

4

•

Getting Started

How to Follow This Programme

HOW TO USE THIS BOOK

This book is for you and your child to use together. But, I do recommend that you read the book from start to finish *before* beginning to use the system it describes with your child. You'll have a better idea of what's involved and how to implement it into your daily lives.

Before beginning, you'll need to discuss the plan of action with your child in detail, explaining that soon they'll be free of this miserable habit – the embarrassment and wet beds.

Traditionally, we've been led to believe that it's better not to discuss bedwetting with our children for fear of upsetting them. In my experience, this is now producing a generation of parents and children who have never acknowledged that it's an unwanted pattern of behaviour. It's easy to move from wearing nappies to night-time pull-ups, the habit is often hushed up and it's quite common for other family members to not even be aware of it.

One mother contacted me after purchasing this book and told me that her 8-year-old daughter was instantly dry at night after the conversation they'd had at the start of this programme. It transpired that her daughter simply hadn't realised that other children no longer wear pull-ups at night and that she should be using the bathroom instead. She was easily able to take control of her bladder and asked her mother why she hadn't said anything sooner!

So, the conversation you'll be having with your child at the start of this programme is a vital part of sowing those seeds of success.

You'll need to get your child's agreement by asking questions such as, *'Does that sound ok to you?'* or *'Are we going to do that?'* as you outline how the programme will work and the commitment that will be required to follow the daily exercises.

Do remember though, that your child may not necessarily think they have a problem that needs fixing in any way, shape or form. Sometimes, it's not even crossed their minds that wearing night-time protective pants is an issue. They may not appreciate you flagging it up as a problem so choose your words carefully and take your time over this.

Just imagine if a neighbour knocked on your front door one day and cheerfully announced that she'd signed you up for your local weight-loss club as she thought it would be good for you. Ouch! All sorts of things would start running through your mind – especially if you'd never discussed your weight with her before and hadn't ever considered yourself to be overweight. The cheek of it!

It's possible to work through this book very quickly, but I'm going to advise that you take at least seven days to allow your child's understanding to deepen. Mark a date on the calendar to indicate the day you will finally rid yourselves of this habit and begin a new life. Better still, get a roll of old wallpaper and stick a large piece of it on your child's bedroom wall – this will give you a blank canvas on which to create a daily diary. Can you think of a date in the future, say a holiday in a couple of months' time, when your child would really want to be dry by? It's good to have an incentive and a key date to be working towards.

(If you prefer you can take up to 14 days to work through all the exercises, but make sure your child is doing at least one activity every day.)

GETTING STARTED

The activities that I've devised are a combination of listening, drawing and visualising. They all serve the same purpose and that is for you and your child to begin creating better pictures in your minds, as this will turn things around for you.

Up until now, your minds have been filled with images of wet sheets, extra laundry, embarrassment and feelings of failure. You probably both have a very good idea of how you don't want things to be and after a while it can become a lot harder to imagine a positive future. These activities are going to make it easier for you.

Having good pictures in our minds is an important step towards achieving success, for human beings are naturally drawn to the ideas in their minds. If the only thoughts and pictures your child has are of wet beds and failures, it's going to be a lot harder to achieve night-time dryness.

EYES-CLOSED AUDIO RECORDING

The first thing you will need to do is to download a special recording called 'Dry Beds Now' from my website at www.stop-bed-wetting-in-7-days.com. This is available free of charge and your child will need to listen to this on a daily basis for at least a week from Day 5 – so get prepared and download it as soon as possible.

Just 20 minutes long, the 'Dry Beds Now' recording is filled with positive suggestions and visualisation exercises to help prepare your child's mind to be receptive to the idea of controlling their bladder at night without having to rely upon protective pants. It's best to provide a quiet time and place without interruptions at some point during the day for your child to do this.

Other downloadable MP3 recordings are available from the website shop: 'Stop Bedwetting Now' (suitable for all ages including teenagers) and 'A Magic Day Out' (a confidence-boosting story for up to age 12). It can be useful to have these additional recordings to keep the momentum of the programme going and provide variety for your child.

Your child can listen to these once they are in bed at night, but during the first couple of days it's good to include some 'daytime' listening too. But please, DO NOT play any of the recordings while you're driving in the car or operating machinery – they're very relaxing and will encourage you to close your eyes! If playing in the car have your child listen through headphones instead.

DRAWING ACTIVITIES

Some of the activities require your child to draw pictures – ensure you have a pad of A4 paper and some felt-tipped pens to hand. I have created some spaces within the book for these, but your child may wish to do some additional drawing. These drawing activities will help with that process of creating good ideas in your child's mind.

The activities should be preceded by a discussion between yourself and your child, so set aside 10–15 minutes for this. During the conversation, you'll be able to get your child thinking on the right track, leaving them to complete the picture afterwards. Encourage your child to tell you about the picture in as much detail as possible – this will ensure that positive ideas cement themselves in their mind.

If your child is older or a teenager, they may prefer to make notes or write their thoughts down in sentences, rather than draw pictures. This will work equally well, for it's the pictures that are being triggered off inside their minds by the drawing or writing activity that are most important here.

VISUALISATION ACTIVITIES

Other activities are visualisation techniques that are, quite literally, eyes-closed imagination games for you to guide your child through. Although fairly simple to do, they have a wonderful effect on helping people achieve their goals. And again, if your child is a teenager then please do reassure them that these types of activities are exactly the same as those done by adults using NLP techniques.

Top golfers, tennis players and footballers regularly use these types of techniques to improve their performance. They 'mentally rehearse' themselves being even more successful in order to improve and really become a winner. Runners see themselves running even faster, footballers see themselves scoring goal after goal. Your body cannot tell the difference between a vividly imagined experience and one that really happened.

Sounds a bit too good to be true, doesn't it? But when footballers practise taking penalties on the training ground, they'll sometimes score goals and sometimes miss. Mistakes become imprinted on the subconscious mind too, so when they play the next match, they'll also remember the bad bits of their training and these will hamper their performance.

The more they practise taking penalties in their imagination, the more successful they'll see themselves being. It's a clever way of tricking the body into feeling that taking great penalties and scoring lots of goals is just something that comes naturally to them.

Now you might be thinking to yourself, 'Oh come on, of course I can tell the difference between an imagined experience and one that happened for real.' So, I'm going to invite you to stop and think for a moment about the last time you saw a scary movie at the cinema.

While your mind knew that what you were watching was only a movie, your body nevertheless responded as if it were happening for real. Your heart probably started to beat a little faster, your breathing became a little shallower, your hands might have begun to feel sweaty and some of you will even have screamed out loud! While you *know* that what you were watching wasn't happening for real, your body nevertheless did *feel* as if it was.

And in just the same way, we're going to be guiding your child through a series of exercises that will enable their body to feel as if it really does have full control over the bladder and that getting up in the middle of the night to visit the bathroom is just one of those things that they can easily do.

Studies show that this kind of 'rehearsal' really does have a positive effect on the outcome. All sorts of magical 'wiring up' takes place in the brain as you practise a scenario over and over – and your child is going to have the opportunity to allow this to happen to them.

It's best to set aside around 15–20 minutes for these visualisation exercises and pick a time when you're unlikely to be interrupted. Providing your child isn't too sleepy, incorporating these activities into their bedtime routine can be ideal.

If your child finds it a little strange to be asked to run through visualisation techniques and imagine things, reassure them that they'll soon get the hang of it. They're doing it all the time already, it's just they hadn't been aware of it.

You can remind them that when they first started to read, they would have been sounding the words in their reading book out loud. And then one day, their schoolteacher would have encouraged them to try 'silent reading', explaining that it's possible to read 'inside your head' without saying the words out loud. Most of us can remember how strange this was to begin with and then slowly, bit by bit, we all learn to read silently to ourselves.

In the same way, your child will learn to 'see' things inside their minds – the pictures are already there, it's just a case of finding them. If your child can draw their ideas on a piece of paper and create pictures, then they are definitely able to visualise.

Remember, this is something that we all do naturally throughout the day. Hairdressers visualise a hairstyle before using their scissors to cut (we hope!) and when we mix ingredients together to bake a cake, we have an idea in our minds of what it will look like when it's finished. We imagine the end result.

These images in our minds are very important, for as human beings we are naturally drawn towards making our reality match our internal pictures. It's like an automatic response that happens so quickly we sometimes feel as if we have no control over it. Understanding how these thought processes work and how they impact our levels of success or failure is the key to helping your child achieve a dry bed.

And it's why I'm going to ask you to guide your child through a series of exercises that will enable them to see themselves having full control over the bladder and walking to the bathroom at night-time.

Tapping into this 'visualisation process' is a safe and natural way to help children overcome their problems.

LEARNING PREFERENCES

We all interpret things in slightly different ways, so one set of instructions will never be interpreted in the same way by different people. Some things always make sense – just not all the time to all of the people. Many teachers now present their school lessons with this in mind. You may have heard them refer to VAK or similar, which stands for visual, auditory and kinaesthetic. I've developed this programme to accommodate these different learning preferences. Some children will find it easier to absorb information by drawing diagrams and pictures, others by listening to the audio recording, and there's also a video programme available for those who find it easier to absorb information by watching it. If you find your child doesn't seem to be making progress, have a think about presenting the information in a different way, rather than giving up.

HAVING 'THAT' CONVERSATION

Before starting this programme, you'll need to have a chat with your child about it. I know that for some of you, this won't be a problem as you're already talking about it, perhaps on a daily basis.

But I also know that others won't have mentioned it at all. After all, you haven't wanted to 'make an issue' out of it or cause any extra embarrassment, so you've simply allowed things to plod along in the hope that they'll somehow resolve themselves.

It can be hard to bring up the subject – but most people find that once things are out in the open, everyone can breathe a sigh of relief. Here are some useful sentences that you can use to get things going. You'll see that these phrases focus on the future and give a sense that things will start to change. Forget the past, focus on a fresh start. I would advise starting the conversation by using words such as 'when' and 'soon', for example:

'When you're ready, you'll be able to visit the bathroom at night rather than wearing these pants.'

'When do you think would be a good time to start?'

'Pretty soon, you won't be needing these pull-ups any more.'

'It won't be long before you can keep yourself dry at night.'

'I don't know exactly when that will be, but I do know that your mind has already started thinking of new ways of doing things.'

'When (the most hypnotic word in the English language) *you're completely dry at night, we'll be able to invite some friends over for a sleepover.'*

And if the idea of having a face-to-face conversation feels tricky, think about having it when you're driving along in the car or walking side by side. For older children and teenagers, you could even consider a late evening stroll outside by torchlight, while star-gazing or looking for nocturnal wildlife. Fostering feelings of closeness will help you discuss tricky problems more easily.

In my work, I've come across families who keep the bedwetting problem a secret from siblings – even when they're sharing a bedroom. One child told me he daren't let his brother know, for they were always squabbling and he knew he'd be teased for it.

I could understand how he was feeling, but at the same time, I wonder whether the secrecy was adding to the tension between the two boys. While the brother may not have been directly told about his sibling's problem, he will have noticed a certain level of collusion between his mother and brother as they had their conversations in hushed tones. When we don't know what's going on, our minds will invent something. Perhaps the brother felt his mother was showing a bit of favouritism towards the other child and felt left out.

And as for the child that's keeping the secret – oh my, the stress of this alone is enough to create wet beds. We'd all like our children to see their home, in particular bedrooms, as a place of safety and security, and this kind of scenario just creates the opposite.

So, it's important to chat with all family members to gather support for the child with the wetting problem. It's time to make it clear that there will be no teasing or shaming. Families stick together and support each other through their problems – while your other children may not have a problem right now, they may well in the future and they'll find that they too would appreciate help and support for it, from those closest to them.

Perhaps the whole family could brainstorm and come up with suggestions of what might help. What problems have they overcome in the past? What did they do that particularly helped?

And while your child is going to be starting this 'behavioural change' programme, what about other members of the family? Are there any other behaviours or habits that anyone else could change at the same time? How about nail-biting, thumb-sucking, being more organised with homework, keeping fit, healthy eating? When you're all changing habits, it helps to take the attention and pressure off the child with the bedwetting problem.

But that's just one way of doing things and you may prefer to do it differently.

It's also going to be a good time to think about whether a certain level of insensitivity has crept into the conversations you've been having with your child. If you've been struggling with stripping beds and washing sheets each morning, before running out of the house for work, then it's only natural that feelings of frustration and exhaustion have started to creep in.

I also know that parents really worry about children who still wet the bed – it's horrible to see our children struggle and only natural that we fear for their futures.

It's time to change your approach to things – taking a step back, along with a deep breath, is the very best thing you can do right now.

Start changing your own behaviour in order to allow change to happen around you.

USING WORDS THAT WORK

'How do I get my kids to listen and do as I tell them?' is probably the question I get asked more than any other.

We all know how frustrating it can be (especially if you're in a hurry) to ask your child to do something, only to have your request fall on seemingly deaf ears. Let's face it, you may as well be speaking to a brick wall. And as soon as frustration creeps into the tone of your voice it makes matters worse and pretty soon things escalate into a battle.

In order to follow this Stop Bedwetting programme, you're going to be asking your child to do several new things, so I'm going to give you a bit of an insight into the 'language of persuasion'. Salespeople, politicians and TV adverts use very persuasive language on us all the time – they encourage us to believe certain things and take the kind of action they'd like us to – and most of the time we don't even realise that they're doing it.

The words that we hear as children have an almost hypnotic effect on our behaviour. How many of us can remember being told that we were not sporty, or that we were useless at maths. Or maybe you were told you were shy, or perhaps always noisy?

How different would our lives have turned out if we'd heard different words?

Sometimes changing just a few words can make all the difference and I'm going to give you some examples to make your life easier.

Say What You Want, Not What You Don't Want

As I mentioned earlier, when we think and speak, our minds are constantly making those all-important images, even if we're not aware of them. Whether you're thinking about phoning a friend or what you need to buy from the shops today, pictures are flashing through your mind all day long.

Because we so often act upon those pictures without really thinking about what we're doing, it's so important to ask your children to do exactly what you want them to do, rather than telling them to *stop* doing something or what you *don't* want them to do.

How many of us have witnessed a young child being told, *'Don't touch the vase!'* only to see them do exactly that? It often leaves parents wondering whether their child is being deliberately defiant, or is deaf perhaps, or just plain stupid!

It happens because there are no pictures for negative words like 'don't', 'no', 'not', 'never', so our minds can only make pictures from the remaining words – which are often what we don't want to have happen. The child could only make a picture from two of the words spoken, 'touch' and 'vase', so it's not surprising that their body took over and they automatically followed the instructions.

So be very careful when you choose your words. Take a look at these examples:

- *'Let's leave the room nice and tidy'*, will produce a different result to saying, *'Don't leave your room in a mess!'*

- *'Let's put our skates on, get dressed super fast this morning and see how much earlier we can get to school today!'* is much more likely to get a child moving than, *'Stop being a slowcoach or we'll be late.'*

- *'Let's walk calmly and slowly'*, is better than, *'Don't run!'*

Now you will understand why so many parents repeatedly groan, *'Why is it you can never do as you're told?'*

So the emphasis throughout this programme is going to be on 'dry beds' rather than not having 'wet beds'. Your language will need to focus on success and staying dry, rather than being wet.

Beware Words That Create Obstacles

Have you ever found yourself struggling to get things done? Have a think about the type of words you use when you speak to yourself. Think of something you've had on your 'to do' list for quite a while and make a sentence out of it, beginning with the words below:

I must...

I should...

I ought to...

I may...

I might...

'I must sort out the cupboards' will not only give you a heavy, negative feeling, but will also be creating a picture in your mind that suggests an uphill struggle. Perhaps you'll get a picture of messy cupboards in your mind.

Whereas, *'I'm going to sort out the cupboards on Tuesday'*, puts a completely different complexion on the matter. Those words are more likely to produce a picture of clean and tidy cupboards in your mind.

'I ought to walk the dog', implies that it's something that you've been putting off doing. The picture that springs to mind might be one of an unwalked dog looking forlorn.

'I want to walk the dog this morning before 11 o'clock', might conjure up an image of you and your dog striding along in the fresh air.

Notice too that I added a couple of extra words the second time around – 'on Tuesday' and 'this morning before 11 o'clock'. Being more specific about your commitment means you are more likely to do it.

So, words to avoid when encouraging your child to follow this programme are:

> You must…
>
> You should…
>
> You have to…
>
> You need to…
>
> You ought to…

Change 'Always' and 'Never' to 'Sometimes'

It's interesting how easy it is to get locked into the idea of failure. Once an idea is firmly established in the mind (e.g. my child is a fussy eater), we unconsciously seek out evidence to support this idea. In other words, it becomes so automatic to remember all the times that food was refused, that we cancel out remembering any moments of success. For example:

- Mealtimes are *always* a struggle.
- My children *never* eat vegetables.
- My children *always* moan when I cook something new.
- Whenever I cook anything new my kids *never* eat it.

Change those *always/never* words into *sometimes* and notice how it changes your feelings.

And in just the same vein, it's easy to fall into the trap of saying that your child *always* wets their bed at night. Is that really true? Have they *never* had a dry night?

I know that for some of you this may possibly be the case, but pretty much all bedwetting children have had the occasional dry night – when staying at Grandma's or at a friend's house perhaps, or during the school holidays following an unusually late night. Often they come out of the blue so it's easy to dismiss occasions like these, believing that they 'don't count'. But they very much do count. These odd random moments of dryness are very important – they are concrete evidence to your child that they can be dry, that they do have the ability to remain dry throughout the night, they just need a little more practise, that's all.

Remember, your words will be creating those all-important pictures inside your child's mind. If your child has been listening to you telling other family members, friends, teachers, doctors, etc. that they *never* have a dry night and that they *always* wet their bed, don't be surprised when they do just that. From now on, it's important to delete those words and use *sometimes* instead.

When going through the programme, remember to record any successes in relation to dry beds that your child has had in the past.

If your child has really never had a dry night, is there any other 'evidence' that you can remember that suggests a degree of success – e.g. staying dry until 5 a.m. or not being 'lifted' on another occasion? It's important to demonstrate to your child that the same thing doesn't always happen every night. Different things do happen *sometimes* – they are not locked into a set pattern of behaviour each and every night.

Give Your Child a Choice

One clever way of steering your child on this programme is to offer the 'illusion' of choice. It will help them to feel more in control of the situation, rather than feeling they're being bamboozled into doing something they haven't chosen to do. Here are some examples:

'Do you want to listen to your audio recording before or after you've had a bath?'

'Which one will you do first? Your visualisation practice or reviewing your notes from yesterday?'

'So, what I'm hearing is you can't start your practice now because there are three things stopping you: you can't find your pencils; you're hungry; and you have your reading homework from school to do. Which of these will you do first, I wonder? You can't do all three at the same time, so choose one first and then move on to the next one.'

A Little Hypnotic Persuasion

It can be really useful to start building hypnotic phrases into your everyday language, for example:

'Now... I'm sure you're wondering how easy it's going to be to make these changes and learn how to keep your bed dry at night.'

'What's good about your wondering is that your mind is already starting to understand what it is it needs to be doing.'

'Everyone learns in this way. And as the ideas we've discussed begin to crystallise into your understanding, it means they'll come naturally to you when you need them.'

'Yes, I understand that it can be a little tricky to begin with... And you'll soon get the hang of it.'

Note the use of 'and' rather than 'but':

'As you stick with this for the next couple of weeks, you'll find it becomes so much easier to keep your bed dry at night. And then you'll know that you can go to sleepovers feeling confident.'

'I already know that you're a really curious person who likes to do new things (give examples, such as riding bikes, swimming, eating olives) *and you'll discover that learning how to keep your bed dry at night is just one more of those things you can successfully do.'*

You can read more about how to help children succeed using the language of persuasion in my book *Words That Work: How to Get Kids to Do Almost Anything* (2015).

GET INTO THE RIGHT STATE

We all know how tough it can be to focus and think clearly when we're feeling stressed. Just think back to the days of taking exams at school and you might remember that horrible feeling of having your mind go blank at precisely the wrong moment. This happens because your body releases stress chemicals such as adrenaline and cortisol and unfortunately these flood the brain, giving you that horrible foggy feeling.

To get the best out of this programme, we're going to want your child's mind to feel open and relaxed, able to think clearly and creatively. That's the best environment for those neural pathways to start doing their work – and it's one of the reasons why I've included the audio download for your child to listen to from Day 5. The sound of my voice, together with the relaxing music, is designed to put your child into a calm state as they listen to the important messages about keeping their bed dry at night.

Some children will approach this programme with enthusiasm and optimism, but I know it's not that easy for everyone. Those who have had a long history of battling this problem, with many hospital visits, a series of alarms and different types of medication under their belt, may be feeling dejected and quite pessimistic. And others who have deadlines to work to, such as an upcoming school residential trip, may already be stuck in a cycle of worry.

It can become increasingly harder to answer questions such as:

> *'What if this happens while I'm away at camp?'*

> *'What if the teacher isn't there?'*

> *'Suppose all my friends see that I've wet my bed, then what?'*

If your child is feeling a bit despondent you've probably already discovered that there's no right thing to say. No matter what answer you give, your child will come back with another concern.

While it's good to talk, endlessly discussing worries can often allow them to become more deeply embedded in your child's mind. Sometimes it's better to say less rather than more – a hug or a cuddle might be better.

You'll find that I'll be introducing some relaxation techniques in the seven-day programme and they will be useful to use on a regular basis.

WHAT TO EXPECT

This bedwetting system has now been used by thousands of children all around the world – so there's plenty of evidence to suggest what is likely to happen once you have followed the seven-day programme.

A *small minority* of you will have instant success – just like the mother and her 8-year-old daughter that I mentioned earlier. For some of you, things will turn around very quickly.

An even *smaller minority* of children might struggle to achieve success and there are some simple reasons for this that can be put right, rather than it being a case of the system not working. I give more information about what you can do in these instances in the 'Frequently asked questions' section at the end of this book.

The overwhelming *majority* of you, however, will get some dry nights in the first week and this will gradually increase over the following two to three weeks. This is usually followed by a period of stabilisation – not every night may yet be dry, but a pattern of dry nights will begin to build up as your child's confidence grows.

It's important to view any wet nights as 'one-off accidents' and not an indication that the system is not working. As already mentioned, these accidents provide valuable learning experiences for your child's mind and if your child has been wetting the bed at night for many *years*, it won't be surprising if it takes a few *days* to get the problem sorted out.

Imagine taking your car, storing it in a garage and locking it away for eight or so years. Would you expect to be able to start it first time on taking it out again? Most probably not – you'd need to do a little tweaking and play around with a few wires and maybe even jump-start it.

It will be a similar experience for getting your child dry at night and all the activities in this book are designed to 'jump-start' the process of having dry nights forever.

Once your child does start getting dry beds for 10–14 consecutive nights then you'll be able to ease off with the daily exercises.

While I do advocate repetition, repetition, repetition as the key to building those new neural pathways, I also appreciate that doing exactly the same thing over and over can become quite tedious. Conscious engagement is what we're aiming for in order to get the best result and if your child starts to 'switch off' and become disheartened, it's time to present the information in a different way.

Josh's Story

Josh is 9 years old and his parents brought him along to see me as he was continuing to be wet every night. Having been referred to their local Enuresis Clinic, they had tried pretty much everything. Alarms did not seem to wake him up and when he was prescribed medication, this just made him urinate even more at night-time. He was wearing pull-ups every night and his parents also woke him up to go to the toilet one last time before they went to bed ('lifting').

They had been trying a variety of methods for over two years with no success. Their doctor suggested they try hypnotherapy as a last resort.

In Josh's school, Year 6 pupils are taken away on a field trip for one week. Josh was beginning to worry – it was becoming more and more important for him to become dry at night, but there did not seem to be a solution.

Josh had two sessions with me – he carried out all the activities and listened to his CD. Rather unusually,

Josh was not dry on the first night, or on the second. By the third night, his parents were ready to abandon things but I persuaded them to stick with it. Josh's habit of night-time wetting was clearly deeply entrenched.

Much to everyone's relief, Josh had a dry night on the fifth night. He continued to have a run of dry nights for over a week before another wet night. This turned out to be a 'one-off' and he went on to have another run of dry nights.

Once in a while, he will have a wet night but overall he has managed to completely change his pattern of night-time behaviour from wet to dry.

I've highlighted this particular case for you because it was a bit trickier to solve. But despite struggling to begin with, it wasn't very long until things just 'clicked' for Josh. 'Sticking with it' proved to be the key to success.

Josh's mum emailed me recently:

Josh has had a further six dry nights in a row and we are all ecstatic. On behalf of all of us, I want to say how grateful we are. Josh seems to be changing too – he seems happier and less moody. It's only now we can see what effect this had on all of us especially Josh – he was becoming so downbeat.

Josh has asked me to say, 'I am very happy it has worked and thank you very much'.

5

•

The Final Countdown

BEFORE YOU BEGIN

To follow this programme there are a few things you will need:

- some sheets of A4 paper

- some felt-tipped pens

- a couple of ordinary party balloons

- a notebook for recording success

- the downloadable audio recording 'Dry Beds Now' from my website

There's a well-known phrase, 'preparation is 90% of success', and I cannot stress strongly enough how being organised and planning in advance could mean the difference between success and failure for your child. Take the time to think about how you are going to manage the whole business of steering your child towards those dry nights.

PICK YOUR MOMENT

Choosing the right moment to introduce this system to your child is key and it's important to pick your moment carefully. Is your child ready to tackle this problem? Do they recognise that it is something that can be dealt with? Do they have a desire to change?

It's not a good idea to pick a week that you know is going to be a particularly busy one with school exams, for example. Likewise, if you know you're going to be away from home for a couple of nights or even going away on holiday it may be best to start this programme at a different time.

The school holidays may prove to be the best time for your child, but for others the lack of routine and late nights may cause more problems. You'll know best which week will be right for you – but do plan ahead.

START KEEPING A DIARY

Before you begin following the programme, I suggest that you keep a diary and record your child's behaviour patterns. After all, if you don't have an exact idea of your starting position then it's going to be harder to identify positive changes. In the busyness of family life, it can be hard to remember what happened on exactly which day. The kind of information that's useful to know is:

- How many times did your child wet last night?

- At what time?

- What kind of a day had it been?

- Was it a busy day at school or perhaps slightly less regimented because of school holidays?

- Had your child had extra sport and become dehydrated?

- Was there lots of homework or anxiety caused by school tests the next morning?

- Was it a late night following a friend's birthday party?

- What did your child eat?

- And how about drinks?

This initial stage should be seen as an information-gathering exercise – it's time to start acting like a detective. The more clues you can pick up on, the more you'll start understanding your child's habit and the easier it will become to help them solve it.

For example, so many children have an accident and wet the bed around 20 minutes before they properly wake up. Could this apply to your child? If so, the solution would be to set an alarm clock to wake your child up in the morning around half an hour earlier than usual. This might mean setting an alarm for around 6 a.m. or even 5.30 a.m., which may seem unpalatable but doing this for a few days might just solve your problem. Usually, once children realise that they not wetting at night and are in fact dry, they feel more confident and find it easier to make the effort to hang on until an acceptable time of the morning.

To make things easier for you, there's a free downloadable 'Stop Bedwetting Diary' that you can download from my website. I suggest printing it off and keeping it somewhere ready to hand.

CLEAR YOUR CLUTTER

Your child is going to be asked to get out of bed and find the route to the bathroom in the middle of the night, should they feel the need to use the toilet. Before doing this, it's worth ensuring that the floor space is completely clear.

Games, toys and piles of dirty clothes that can be tripped over will not add to your child's confidence about their ability to make it to the bathroom in the dark. A cluttered, disorganised room will reflect your child's cluttered, disorganised mind and this is not going to help.

Parents can often find getting children to tidy their rooms a bit of a challenge. Be patient with your child and take the time to help them sort things out. Reluctance to tidy a bedroom can seem like 'laziness' but in fact children can often find it difficult to visualise a tidy room and if they can't see it in their imaginations, they won't be able to create it in reality.

Once your child's room is neat and tidy, it's worth taking a few photographs and leaving them in the room as reference points. In the future, you can simply ask your child to make their room look just like it did in the photo.

Avoid using phrases like, *'Don't leave your room in a mess'*, because this will only create pictures in their minds of a messy room and it will be very much harder for them to tidy it up. Using sentences like, *'Let's see if we can get the room nice and tidy'*, will be much more helpful to them. Always say what you *do* want to have happen, rather than what you *don't* want.

TOO LIGHT OR TOO DARK?

Some children who come to see me will often reveal in a session that they 'would go to the bathroom at night, only it's too dark'. Would this apply to your child?

Check that the route to the bathroom is well lit. However, while it's important to have enough light outside the bedroom so they can find their way, I would recommend having less light inside the bedroom. Sleep experts agree that night lights are best switched off as your child begins to grow up. Your child will experience a deeper, better quality sleep if the room is dark and this alone may ensure a dry night.

It is now possible to buy night lights with motion sensors – they are only activated when they sense movement, i.e. someone getting out of bed. This could be a better solution to your problem.

If your child really is too scared to visit the bathroom, you could consider placing a potty next to the bed. It may be easier for them just to step out of bed to relieve themselves and once the satisfaction and delight of dry beds has been achieved, you may find their confidence levels are boosted enough for the next step. Of course, this does depend entirely on your personal preference and the age of your child. For some children, this is a useful 'halfway' measure and it achieves the aim of getting that bed dry.

BATHROOM

And what about the bathroom or toilet? One child who came to see me admitted that he was scared to go to the loo at night because of 'the black toilet seat' – it was the first his mother knew of this. It wasn't so much a case of not wanting to admit it sooner, it really hadn't occurred to him to speak up about it until he started talking to me. It's worth taking the time to make the bathroom as child-friendly as possible.

Position as many items as possible at child height – e.g. mirrors, towel rails, soap and even small wash-hand basins if possible.

Allowing your child to choose some of the accessories, such as colourful hand towels, will help your child to feel that this space belongs to them as much as to the adults in the house.

DOUBLE-VOIDING

I've suggested something called 'double-voiding' to a number of children now and it does seem to help. Double-voiding involves going to the toilet *twice* just before going to sleep.

Most children will visit the toilet last thing at night and then spend an extra 20–30 minutes getting ready for bed or reading a story. Others rush in and out of the loo so quickly that they don't fully empty their bladders.

Either way, asking your child to go back into the bathroom a second time before tucking down for the night ensures that their bladder is completely empty and does seem to help with staying dry all night.

DEEP SLEEPERS

I'm often told by parents that their children are such deep sleepers that they simply do not wake up at night and so it's not possible for them to take themselves to the bathroom at night.

My response to this is 'beware the self-fulfilling prophecy'. Yes, there are some children who are out for the count and nothing will seem to rouse them from a deep, deep sleep – not even lying in a soaking wet bed.

However, it never ceases to amaze me the number of times I have worked with one of these 'deep sleepers' and had them admit to me that they are in fact aware of wetting their beds – that they do momentarily wake up but they just can't bring themselves to get up and go to the bathroom. Various excuses are then given – they are either slightly afraid (something the parent wasn't aware of, even if steps had been taken to avoid this) or it was simply too cold to contemplate getting out of bed. After the event, they simply fall back asleep.

I know for many children, the biggest obstacle they face is sleeping in a bunk or cabin-style bed. One child I worked with slept at the top of a triple-decker bed as he had two younger siblings sleeping beneath him. Clambering out of bed when half-asleep was, understandably, a step too far for him.

If this sounds like a familiar problem, consider placing a mattress on the floor for the duration of this programme. You'll quickly see if this is the real cause of the bedwetting and not simply a case of 'deep sleeping'.

But in any event, I say 'beware the self-fulfilling prophecy' because if being a deep sleeper is your child's problem, they may well have overheard you repeating this 'deep sleep' mantra many times over, either within the family unit or to any of the health professionals that you've visited in the past.

For years your child could have been hearing that they are a deep sleeper and nothing will wake them up. A nice hypnotic suggestion if ever I heard one! I wonder how different things could be right now if all your child had ever heard was what a *light sleeper* they were and how easy it was for them to get up at night and go to the bathroom!

The truth is, we all know that it's very easy to programme our minds to wake up at a specific time. How many times in the past have you had to wake up at some ridiculous hour of the morning to go on holiday? Most of us will go to bed worrying about oversleeping only to find ourselves waking up two minutes before the alarm clock goes off. And then we feel strangely spooked by it!

Many children are just as good at programming themselves to wake up extra early – Christmas morning and birthdays in particular. The prospect of receiving presents is enough to get them jumping out of bed really early in the morning. Without even realising it, they programmed their minds to wake up early the night before.

And as you'll discover in this programme, it's going to be possible to do the same with waking up to go to the bathroom and avoiding that accident.

FAMILY TREES

I'm often asked if bedwetting runs in families. Many of the parents who come to see me tell me that they were bedwetters until quite late and grandparents can confirm that other members of the family were too.

There's often a desire to trace back through generations and pinpoint the bedwetters in the family and I can understand this as part of your quest to find a reason for your child's problem.

However, I can tell you that I come across far more bedwetting children *without* a family history than I do children *with*. Perhaps there is a link, but for many there simply isn't.

Again, I worry about the self-fulfilling prophecy here. If your child repeatedly overhears conversations in the family of all the generations before them who had this problem, it's going to be very much harder for them to change. Their self-image (the way that they view themselves) is going be distorted by the evidence that is presented to them of all these bedwetting relatives.

There have been occasions when parents have opened a session with me by saying, 'I wet the bed until I was 10, so I guess it's going to be the same for my son'. And if the child that is overhearing this is only 7 years old, it's very likely that he's not going to fix his problem any time soon.

So, my advice to you is that it doesn't really matter if Auntie Clara, Cousin Jim, 'Uncle Tom Cobley and all' wet their beds too. It's irrelevant. The only person who is important right now is your child. They are a wonderful, unique human being and have the resources and capability to be the master of their own destiny.

It can be helpful to reassure your child by letting them know that they're not alone and that it has happened to other members of the family, but follow this up by saying that they weren't lucky enough to have the benefit of programmes such as this one to help them stop it quickly.

CHANGING DRINKING HABITS

There's conflicting advice regarding how many drinks a child who is trying to stop bedwetting should or shouldn't have each day.

Some experts recommend children drink more water during the day to allow the bladder to stretch and get used to accommodating more liquid at night. Others will recommend restricting drinks and certainly none at all after about 4.30 p.m.

But then again, some feel that constipation may be one of the reasons for bedwetting – and they would advocate increasing fluids throughout the day.

It's no wonder parents can feel confused.

Personally, I'm not in favour of restricting fluids in young children and certainly not on hot summer days. I feel common sense should prevail – if your child is thirsty, they should be able to have a drink.

If your child has been encouraged to drink more during the day, they may have got into the habit of gulping and drinking too quickly.

Remind them that early evening drinks should be sips of water only and not the huge quantities they may have got used to drinking during the day.

Some of the children who have followed my programme noticed that they were more likely to have a wet bed if they'd had too many sugary, fizzy drinks (including fruit juices) or caffeinated drinks (such as cola, chocolate, tea or coffee) the day before. So, my advice would be 'keep it simple' – let's stick to plain water wherever possible but don't make a big deal of it.

CHANGING EATING HABITS

Did you know that eating certain foods can also have an effect on the bladder? Perhaps you've experienced the changes in the smell and colour of your own urine after eating asparagus or beetroot, for example?

Water-based fruits and vegetables such as strawberries, melon, grapes, celery and artichokes have a diuretic effect on the body – they encourage you to expel water! I have come across many parents who substitute evening drinks with pieces of fruit so be careful, because you could be causing problems rather than solving them.

It's also known that eating too much wheat can cause a sensitivity in the bladder – while the effects are not necessarily noticeable on the outside, the inside of the bladder can become slightly inflamed and as a result make you want to wee more often.

We've become a society that's very dependent on eating a lot of wheat-based products – it's worth thinking about your child's diet and if you find that they eat cereal or toast for breakfast, followed by sandwiches for lunch and then pizza or pasta for dinner, consider making some changes or at least keeping a food diary to see if you can make a connection between the food your child eats and wet nights.

While I'm not in the habit of suggesting exclusion diets, I do think it's worth experimenting for a period of two weeks and cutting out all wheat. Substitute this with more rice or potatoes. Evening meals could consist of jacket potatoes or even chips! Remember, it's just an experiment and is not a regime that your child will follow forever.

It's also been suggested to me by some doctors that milk could be the cause of bedwetting and very often I find that children who come to see me still drink milk at night-time or have had some sensitivity to it in the past.

Another big culprit is the use of artificial sweeteners as they too can have a diuretic effect. These are often hidden in children's food and drinks under the guise of 'healthy' eating, so it's easy not to notice if your child is consuming these. Beware any drinks or fruit squash that are sugar-free and also yoghurt, fromage frais or ice cream that is low in sugar and labelled 'good for children's teeth' or 'low calorie'. Go through all your cupboards and read the labels carefully. Eliminate these from your child's diet now.

And, rather confusingly, real sugar can also be the cause of wet beds. Most parents would agree that sweet, fizzy drinks will result in a bad night.

Once your child has established a run of dry nights, it won't be surprising if from time to time they have the odd wet night. This will be the perfect time to think back over the previous 24 hours and analyse their food and drink intake to see if you can track down the reason.

Most parents tell me that whenever their children go to a birthday party, they know that they're going to be in for a bad night with several wet beds. It's not surprising given that they've probably consumed just about every known trigger food and drink in the space of a few hours.

One child who came to see me couldn't understand why he'd been dry for several weeks and then during the Christmas holidays had wet his bed several times. 'It always happens when I go to Grandma's', he told me. A little further questioning revealed that Grandma loved grapes and each time he visited her they would sit together in front of the TV eating whole bunches at a time.

If you do find a connection between your child's bedwetting and certain foods, it may be worth consulting a qualified nutritionist who can carry out further tests and help devise suitable menus.

CONSTIPATION

I've mentioned that constipation is a very common cause of bedwetting – an overly full bowel will rest heavily against the bladder at night encouraging it to empty, perhaps even before your child has had a chance to feel the urge the go. And the more the bowel pushes against the bladder, the less room there is for holding urine.

It's not always easy to know whether your child is constipated – once they become independent, we tend to leave them to it rather than follow them to the toilet, so we can only go by what they tell us.

Once they start school, it's not uncommon for children to avoid doing a poo at school – it's embarrassing to do this among friends and the toilets may not be all that welcoming.

Here's what I suggest – visit my website (www.stop-bed-wetting-in-7-days.com) and you'll find something called the 'Bristol Stool Guide'. Developed at the Bristol Royal Infirmary in 1997, it's a diagnostic medical tool designed to classify human poo into seven categories ranging from severe constipation to severe diarrhoea.

Put simply, this chart has seven pictures of different types of poo. If you're a bit squeamish you may not want to look, but they are quite friendly drawings rather than real photos, so not that bad really.

Children love these types of things and I would recommend you download the chart, print it off and stick it up on the bathroom wall. Then create a diary and stick it up next to the chart and ask your child to note down which picture most resembles the type of poo they've just passed. Gradually you'll start getting a clearer picture of whether constipation could the cause of your bedwetting problems.

This chart is also useful because it has diagrams showing the optimum seating positions when sitting on the toilet. It may be that your child would be more comfortable and find it easier to use the toilet with a small step to rest their feet on.

Many health professionals and doctors prescribe laxatives such as Movicol for bedwetting children and if your child has a severe problem then this may be the solution.

But I'm a great believer in the positive effects of probiotics – the healthy bacteria that we should all have a good supply of in the gut. If your child has been unwell recently and needed to take a course of antibiotics then their supply of good bacteria will be depleted. Antibiotics are great for killing bad bacteria but they also wipe out good bacteria. Getting a healthy supply back into the system will help to correct your child's bowel habits. The brand I recommend is Bio-Kult – check out their website as their Infantis product is suitable for children.

DIGITAL DETOX

I am not a great fan of TVs and computers in children's bedrooms. Nowadays it's easy to become overloaded with devices – mobile phones, TVs, gaming machines, computers, tablets, etc. and if they're plugged in and left to charge overnight, it's particularly unhealthy.

Scientific experts agree that sleeping in an electromagnetic field does not aid restful sleep. Looking at screens an hour or so before bedtime makes it harder to fall asleep and interferes with melatonin production – the hormone that induces sleepiness. There's a part of me that still wonders if children are perhaps not falling into the correct sleep patterns at night-time and if they were, bedwetting would be less likely to occur.

I recommend clearing the 'energy space' in your child's bedroom as much as possible by removing as many electrical items as you can.

The visualisation techniques in this book are designed to help your child's brain make new neural connections and wire itself up in a different way. This will be taking place as your child sleeps and dreams – the less interference the better. Playing exciting computer games or watching TV for a short while before going to sleep will add to the confusion in your child's mind just at the moment when it will be needed the most.

It can be hard for today's parents to set rules and boundaries around screen time, but it certainly helps to get clear on what is and is not acceptable. Be sure your child knows and understands the rules and why you're setting limits.

You can find extra help for tackling screen-time issues in another one of my books, *Words That Work: How to Get Kids to Do Almost Anything* (2015). Here you'll learn why I don't recommend using daily time limits to control your child's screen habits.

STAYING POSITIVE

It's important to remain encouraging and enthusiastic throughout this process. Remember, the more confident you appear, the more likely your child is to be successful.

Praise your child regularly and be sympathetic if they have an accident one night. Remind your child that sticking to the exercises will ensure that they have dry nights forever.

For a lot of children, following this programme may mean the situation is going to get worse before it gets better. If your child has been wearing some form of night-time protection all their life, this is potentially the first time they will ever have experienced a wet bed. It's not pleasant; it's uncomfortable and it's disruptive.

It's important that you stay strong for your child during this time. Remember, if you do not take the initiative to help solve this problem, your child could be stuck with it for many, many years to come.

We all need a bit of motivation to change the habits in our lives – think back to the last time you wanted to make changes in your life: lose weight, quit smoking or take up exercise for example. You probably thought about doing something for quite a while before you actually got to the point of taking action. Something tipped you over the edge and spurred you into action. It could be the same for your child.

I was contacted by one father who worried because his son had really lost his temper one night – he had kicked his wardrobe door and sobbed, 'I'm so fed up with all of this!'

I reassured the father that this was actually a good sign. And sure enough, one week later I received an email telling me that the boy had been dry every night since.

Think about it, when life is too comfortable there is no incentive for any of us to make changes, why would we bother? And in just the same way, if your child never experiences a degree of discomfort, their mind will find it much harder to register what 'success' looks and feels like.

A fairy godmother isn't going to fly through your child's bedroom window at night, wave her wand and make your child magically dry at night. It's going to take persistence and training of the right sort. Keeping dry at night is a really important life skill that your child needs to acquire and you are doing absolutely the right thing by putting them on this training path to success.

Too often I have found that parents give in just at the point at which their child was about to turn things around for themselves. Have trust and faith in your child's ability to work through this problem – all you need to do is support them.

Remember, your child is going to encounter many disappointments and failures in their life – we all do. Your child will not pass every single exam they sit and nor will everyone they meet instantly take a liking to them. Learning how to deal with disappointments by dusting yourself down, picking yourself back up and striving for success once more is going to be one of the very best life lessons your child can learn.

In fact, being a bedwetter could prove to be to your child's *advantage*, rather than *disadvantage* in life. So many times, I've watched children who have used this system to fix their bedwetting go on to use the same techniques and approach to achieve success in other areas of their life – be it in the classroom, on the sports field or even onstage.

DITCHING THE NIGHT-TIME PULL-UP PROTECTIVE PANTS

I know many of you will still be using nappies or waterproof absorbent pants at night-time. Naturally, common sense has been telling you to keep using them until your child becomes dry at night – why wouldn't you? But as I've already explained, this creates an obstacle for those vital signals that need to be travelling between the bladder, your child's skin and the brain. The pants also offer no incentive for your child to keep themselves dry at night and encourage them to see themselves as a bedwetter, believing that there's simply nothing they can do about it.

Health professionals now agree that it's best to stop using them from around the age of 6. From this time, it's better for your child to feel the wetness and learn how to cope with it.

I agree with this, however, I'd rather you didn't make your child go 'cold turkey' and ditch the pants overnight. My programme will help you to prepare your child for this event, by helping them to understand more about the problem and become creative at finding solutions, as well as boosting their confidence. As you will see, I recommend removing the protective pants from Day 5 – forever! By preparing for this event, the possibility of having a dry night will be increased.

If you're reading this and have a child that has already stopped using pants and you're used to dealing with wet beds each night, don't worry about having missed out a step. Your child's motivation to get this problem solved will likely be higher as being wet is not only embarrassing, but also hugely inconvenient (for both of you).

LIFTING

Parents are commonly encouraged to rouse their child from sleep later in the evening, just as they're going to bed themselves. They then carry their child off to the bathroom, pop them on the loo and encourage them to have one last wee before going back to bed again.

On the face of it, it sounds like a good idea. Surely, this is common sense – your child's bladder is small and having a late night toilet visit will increase the chances of a dry bed in the morning.

However, I'm not convinced that this is a good idea at all. First of all, it's not a particularly pleasant experience – would you like to be woken in the middle of the night and dragged off to the bathroom? It can trigger off a battle of wills and make it much harder for you to discuss the bedwetting habit and get your child to be an active and co-operative participant in the getting dry process.

Second, I think it's important to remember what the real goal of this exercise is. Your goal is to help your child achieve night-time dryness. By introducing the 'lifting' method you are doing the exact opposite of what you're hoping to achieve. You are actively *training* your child to release urine when they are half-asleep and also develop a need to go to the toilet in the middle of the night. We know how easy it is for habits to develop, and it only needs a couple of weeks of taking your child to bathroom at 11 p.m. for their bodies to automatically expect this to happen. However well intentioned, it's not helpful to the process so I recommend leaving it out.

And if you've already implemented this strategy, please don't despair. From time to time I do get contacted by parents who feel dreadfully guilty as they tell me, 'I've read your book and can see that I've done it all wrong! It's all my fault.'

Well no – it isn't your fault and you're not a bad parent. You followed the advice that well-meaning people, including many health professionals, gave you. Lifting may work for some people, but I'm guessing it hasn't worked for you – because you're reading this book, right? So, the fact that you tried one way to help your child and are now changing tack and seeking out alternatives makes you a great parent and not a bad one.

DEALING WITH ACCIDENTS

So, it is possible that your child will be dry *every* night from Day 7 of this programme, but it's probably unlikely. Planning in advance will make any accidents much easier to deal with. Have plenty of spare sheets and bedding as well as a plastic protective cover for the mattress.

Consider making up the bed with two layers of sheets and placing an absorbent mat or pad in between these layers. If your child does wet the bed in the middle of the night, you'll be able to quickly remove the top sheet together with the absorbent pad, giving you a ready-made dry bed for them to climb into quickly. Alternatively, you could simply position a bath towel over the wet patch and tell your child to sleep on top of this. This will minimise night-time disruptions.

Other useful products include waterproof outer liners for duvets and inner liners for sleeping bags. These in particular are useful for sleepovers as they not only keep the bag dry, but also the bed or even the carpet if they happen to be sleeping on the floor.

This period of adjustment should only last a few weeks, so consider organising extra help for yourself if you feel you'll need it. Could wet bedding be sent to the local laundry for example? Could you purchase some extra linen cheaply, to give you plenty of spares to use? The easier you can make life for yourself at this moment, the better 'support partner' you'll be for your child.

Your child is going to need you to stay positive, confident and relaxed with them as you work through this system. Don't let something like a few wet sheets spoil this for you all.

It's a good idea to encourage your child to play a part in changing any wet beds. Some parents groan when they hear this as they have got into the habit of clearing up after their child and worry that getting them involved will be met with resistance, but it's an important part of the process of learning how to take responsibility for yourself.

If your child is still quite young, this can be kept to stripping off the wet sheet and putting it in the laundry basket, with an adult finishing things off for them. This is not designed to be a punishment, in the 'you made a mess – you clear it up' vein, but it definitely does help the penny to drop quicker if your child can accept responsibility for the wetness and 'ownership' of the problem. They'll start understanding the consequences of not keeping control of their bladder – as they strip off the bed, that little voice will be chatting away inside their heads, enabling them to think a bit harder about the how, what and why of their problem.

I always tell children that the 'good thing' about problems that we 'own' is that we can find solutions for them much more easily. For example, if a dog walked past your front garden each morning and decided to have a wee against the gate, it's going to be quite hard to get it to change its behaviour. It's not that easy to change someone or something else. The good thing about your child's bedwetting is that they cause it to happen. And things that you 'start' you can also 'stop'. We can all take control of our own problems.

If asking your child to change sheets every time they're wet seems a bit too much to ask of them, how about picking just two days each week? Negotiate with your child by telling them that you'll be happy to be on 'sheet duty' for five days each week if they take the other two days. Then ask your child to pick which days they think will be the best for them to be on duty, e.g. weekends or a midweek day when they're not in a rush to get to school.

Having a calendar in the room that reminds them when it's their turn is also a good way of seeing how much they're able to programme their minds to produce a dry night. If your child is always dry when it's their turn to change the sheets, but has a wet night when it's your turn, you'll know you're on to something!

Some children admit to being a bit too lazy to get out of bed to go to the bathroom at night and often asking them to help out with sheet changing is enough to tip the balance. Let's face it, it's easier to nip to the bathroom than change the sheets on a bed!

REWARD SYSTEMS AND PUNISHMENTS

I imagine that most parents will know that doling out punishments, introducing consequences (such as losing pocket money) or getting angry are of no benefit when it comes to changing a child's habits and behaviours with regard to bedwetting and should not be used. If only it were that simple. No child wants to hang on to this problem – if they could have stopped sooner, they would have done so. When we feel unhappy and stressed it becomes much harder to make changes. Sure, I get it – you're exhausted given the lack of sleep, mountains of washing and most of all, you're worried about your child. But things need to change now and that change can start with you – it's time to take a deep breath and start looking at this problem through a different pair of eyes.

Now, if we're not going to use negative consequences, it may surprise you to learn that I'm also not in favour of reward systems.

On the face of it, some sort of recognition in the form of a coveted item does sound like a good idea and offering a carrot may well make all the difference to your child's level of motivation.

However, rewarding and praising children has grown in popularity to such a degree that few of us stop to question whether it's actually a good idea. But studies do show that when children expect or anticipate rewards, they can actually end up performing worse.

A well-known experiment carried out by the psychologist Edward L. Deci featured two groups of students who were invited to work on an interesting puzzle. One half of the group was paid to do this and for the other half there was no reward involved.

It was discovered that the group who received no payment ended up being significantly keener to continue to play with the puzzle in their free time. They also showed more enthusiasm for the task and were able to engage with it more and as a result were more successful. The other group was clearly more focused on the financial reward and as a result they did all that was asked of them and no more.

Over the years, many other similar experiments have been carried out that back up this theory. It's easier to engage with an activity if there's no distraction of a reward.

Stop for moment and think about your feelings towards your work and your hobbies. Why is it that we can struggle to get up in the mornings for work, but find it so much easier to bounce out of bed to pursue a hobby? There's a different sense of pleasure and success to be derived from a task if there's no distracting element of a reward.

Of course, there has to be something positive to be gained out of any kind of task otherwise there would be no point in doing it. But encouraging your child to keep the end goal in sight as the 'reward' is going to increase their chances of getting there.

I appreciate this might be going against advice that you'll have received from other sources – star charts, for example, are often recommended for bedwetting problems. It's great to receive a shiny, golden star on your chart, but what happens if you have a wet night? Not only is your bed wet, but now you're not going to receive a star either. Double negative.

It's fine to keep a chart on the wall to monitor progress – this is not a bad idea, but rather than sticking stars, encourage your child to fill in some extra details such as what worked well, what could be improved and what needs changing for the next day.

This doesn't mean that your child should never get a treat again – but a treat is not the same as an enticement. So, having a day trip out to a theme park to celebrate the end of the school year and the hard work put in to get through exams is a great idea.

But it's not the same as saying, 'Work hard at your exams and I'll give you X amount of money for each "A" grade and take you to the theme park.' This only adds to the pressure – and what are you going to do if the grades are not so good?

I always felt that if any of my children got bad grades at school, they were probably *more* in need of a day trip out to let off steam, not less. Once you start 'rewarding', it follows that you have to start 'unrewarding' and that's just not enjoyable parenting.

The reward in this process is going to be those elusive dry beds. Your child will begin to feel so much happier, more confident and relaxed with stress-free sleepovers and school trips to look forward to. That is a huge bonus and we want them to keep picturing this in their minds, for as I've explained, this is hugely instrumental in creating the difference between success and failure. We don't want any brain power to be diverted off in the direction of extra pocket money, sweets or new trainers. Stay focused on the job in hand – and do your celebrating later.

HOW TO PRAISE USING WORDS THAT WORK

We've all heard that we should praise our children frequently to build up their self-esteem and encourage them to ditch bad habits and behave well. It's not uncommon, however, to run out of words to use and so most parents, and indeed teachers, find themselves stuck with a limited vocabulary and use words such as:

> wonderful
>
> well done
>
> amazing

brilliant

fantastic

clever

As well-intentioned as this kind of superlative praise can seem, these words quickly lose their meaning if used too often and end up sounding a little fake. When running my Montessori school, it was even more important for me and my teachers to be aware of this. You can imagine a scenario where 26 children are lining up ready to go home – if the teacher tells each child that the piece of artwork they're taking home is 'fantastic' or 'brilliant', it's going to become obvious to the child that it's an automatic response and not a genuine compliment.

In just the same way, it's easy to fall into the trap of using the wrong words in response to a mediocre performance, which can leave your child slightly confused, wondering if they are in fact able to do any better – as would happen if you showered your child with praise for having a slightly wet bed rather than a sopping wet one. It's going to be more important to praise the effort and the intention, rather than the outcome, as this will increase your child's motivation and their willingness to overcome challenges.

Begin by noticing and commenting on exactly what your child has done that is right or just ok. This is quite literally 'saying what you see'.

For example:

'Even though you weren't completely dry last night, I can see that you're taking the time to think about the changes you're starting to make.'

'I can see that you put a lot of effort into taking off your wet sheets and getting your bed ready for tonight. That's very helpful – thank you. You're heading in the right direction.'

'I told you it was time for bed and you came straight up into the bathroom. You're clearly determined to get things right.'

This kind of dialogue shows your child that you're paying attention, noticing what they're doing and that you appreciate their efforts. This is a much better way of engaging with your child and elevating their feelings of confidence.

Some useful sentence starters include:

'You've been remembering to…'

'I hear you…'

'I've noticed…'

'In the past week, you…'

'Nowadays you usually…'

'I can see that you…'

CONSIDER FINDING A 'BUDDY'

As a mother of three children, I'm all too familiar with the feelings of frustration at being on the receiving end of a child's reluctance to carry out simple tasks, especially if they then willingly perform them for their teachers and tutors. If you feel yourself becoming caught up in a similar situation with this system, then consider using a 'buddy'. This could be a trusted family friend, uncle or aunt, or even a teacher – someone who the child could speak to and liaise with on a regular basis.

Of course, the two of you will still have to be working together with regards to the overall plan to stop bedwetting, but it may help you to find someone else to carry out the programme's exercises with them.

It is also possible to purchase an online video version of this Stop Bedwetting programme – further details are on the website.

Rather than working through the homework exercises using this book, your child can watch daily short video clips where I do the talking and explaining. In essence, I'll do the work for you and it's similar to the experience your child would have if they were in a private one-to-one consultation with me.

It's a good option to consider if you and your child have struggled with this problem for some time and you're at the stage where it's hard to have a conversation about it without things becoming a little heated.

A FINAL WORD

Throughout this book, I've used some well-known hypnotic phrases and sentences – just as I would if you were sitting in a face-to-face session with me. These words are designed to help you see a successful future and feel pumped up and motivated, ready to face your challenge.

It's important to remember that while you will have had the benefit of reading these words, your child has not – unless you decide your child is old enough to read this book and work through the exercises independently.

So, my advice is to spend plenty of time discussing the ideas in this book with your child before you begin – your child's thought processes will need time to 'catch up' with yours. By all means, repeat some of the words that you've been reading here and get in the habit of using them.

6

•

The Golden Rules

Remember to follow these golden rules:

1. Before you begin, read this book in its entirety and familiarise yourself with the process.

2. Get organised with sheets of paper, pens, balloons, audio recording and waterproof bedding.

3. Start keeping a diary to get as many clues as possible about your child's behaviour. Start acting like a detective.

4. Monitor your child's eating, drinking and toilet habits.

5. Have the all-important conversation with your child and the rest of the family and consider reading my book *Words That Work*.

6. Pick the right moment to begin this programme. Mark a date in the calendar.

7. Clear the bedroom clutter.

8. Check lighting levels.

9. Have a digital detox.

10. Ensure the bathroom is inviting and access to it is clear.

11. Change sleeping arrangements if needs be.

12. Phase out any 'lifting' routines that you've been using.

13. Ensure you'll be able to deal with night-time wetting accidents efficiently. Discuss the protocol with your child.

14. Review my advice about rewards and punishments.

15. Stay positive and take steps to look after your own welfare too – your child needs you to be feeling strong.

16. Consider finding a buddy.

7
.
Before We Begin

HOW TO FOLLOW THIS PROGRAMME

There are a few preliminary activities for you and your child to do before getting started and you can spend a few days in this preparation/thinking stage.

While the activities that follow have been packaged up into a seven-day programme, it is fine to take a little longer. There will be days when you have a busy schedule and less time to follow the homework activities. However, I would recommend that you take no longer than 10–14 days as you'll start to lose momentum if gaps appear too often. And second, I would recommend it's also important that you do a little bit of something each day. So even if you don't have time to do the homework exercise on a particular day, try to have a meaningful conversation or have one of the audio recordings playing as you travel in the car with your child listening through headphones, or as your child is getting ready for bed, for example.

DIARY KEEPING

As I mentioned earlier, it's important to take stock of where you are with regards to your child's bedwetting habit. You'll need to record your starting position so any progress you make can be seen more clearly.

You can either use a blank notebook, the 'Stop Bedwetting in Seven Days Diary', which is available to download for free from the website, or you can keep notes electronically on a phone or tablet.

Start by making a note of what your child eats and drinks and at what time of the day. Then, make a note of what happens during the day, for example:

- a regular school day

- exams or homework

- extra sports or exercise

- birthday party or play date

- food and drinks consumed

- toilet habits

- away on holiday

- bad night's sleep or nightmares

- sickness or illness

- time they went to bed

- time they woke up in the morning

And then, remember to record what happened at night-time – how many times is your child wet? At what time? How did you deal with wet sheets? Was your child involved in the clearing up?

Tell your child that from now on, you'll both be behaving like detectives searching for clues as to what might be triggering this problem and how it can be solved.

BUILDING A POSITIVE SELF-IMAGE

It's not unusual for children who have a history of wetting their beds at night to have a poor self-image. This is especially so if the problem has continued for many years.

However hard parents may have tried to minimise the negative impact, it won't have escaped the child's attention that their lives are full of wet, smelly pants or sheets and that they can't quite enjoy all of the things that most other children do, such as having sleepovers easily with their friends.

If other methods to solve the bedwetting problem, such as the use of alarms, medication or lifting, have also been tried with no success, this will just add to the child's perception of themselves as a failure.

It's really important to reinforce your child's perception of themselves as a good, worthwhile, confident and successful person. The more you can build up this image, the more likely your child is to be successful. The pictures we create in our minds with our imaginations play a very big part in determining what happens in our lives.

Step 1

Ask your child to make a list of things that they feel they are good at or found relatively easy to learn. For example, writing their name, learning to read, taking care of a pet, baking a cake, singing, dancing or playing musical instruments – these can be as varied and as simple or complicated as they like.

Things I am good at:

. . . .

. . . .

. . . .

. . . .

. . . .

. . . .

. . . .

Step 2

Now ask your child to list activities that they struggled with initially, but eventually mastered. For example, things that were a little trickier to learn, such as riding a bike, swimming, writing their name or learning to read.

Things I had to practise before I became successful:

. . . .

. . . .

. . . .

. . . .

. . . .

. . . .

. . . .

Remind Your Child

Once upon a time, they couldn't walk and couldn't talk, or even feed themselves, but gradually over time these were new things that they learnt and can now do quite easily. And the older your child, the longer the list of things that they have mastered in their lives is going to be.

Having dry beds is just one more of those things that they will easily learn.

And if your child has siblings, is there something they struggled with at first too, but gradually mastered? And what about yourself? Is there anything you've got better at? If so, you could mention this too – demonstrating that we all struggle to learn new things, so your child is not alone. Fortunately, humans are very clever and when we practise things over and over, we eventually become really good at them.

Step 3

I'm pretty sure that getting dry at night won't be the only thing that's a work in progress in your child's life right now. Write down 'getting dry at night' and then add a couple more to the list. For example, learning backstroke, learning how to play football, memorising the times tables. Emphasise the fact that we're all learning how to do new things all of the time.

Things I'm still learning to do:

. . . .

. . . .

. . . .

. . . .

. . . .

. . . .

. . . .

Do take your time over these activities. You may want to spend a few days to think them through rather than rushing and doing them in five minutes. As your child thinks about the questions and completes the answers, a picture will slowly build up in their mind – and this will help to create the difference between success and failure.

8

·

Day 1

My New Future

Welcome to Day 1 of this life-changing programme for your child. You can spend a few moments reviewing and discussing the preliminary activities. Perhaps your child will have thought of a few more ideas to add in to their lists.

STEP 1: MY NEW FUTURE – WHAT WILL IT BE LIKE?

Today, I'd like you to invite your child to take a glimpse into the future: that wonderful future when everything is just the way they would like it to be… waking up each morning with a dry bed.

Begin by asking:

What will you see?

What will you feel?

What will you hear?

Ask your child to draw a picture showing how fantastic waking up in the morning will be. This is an important step towards getting them to be able to visualise a new future clearly. Without this, it will be much harder for them to achieve success.

Include as much information as possible – the bed with dry sheets, the time and perhaps even what the weather is like outside.

Ask your child to remember to include themselves in the picture with a big smile on their face. They can add in other people, perhaps having them speaking some words. Encourage your child to write a sentence at the bottom of the picture along the lines of, for example:

> *It is* _____ (fill in the important date you've chosen to be dry by) *and I'm waking up with a dry bed. I see my nice, clean dry sheets and other people smiling because they're pleased for me. I feel happy and confident and I hear myself whoop with delight.*

You can play around with the details in this sentence to suit, but the words should reflect how bright and shiny the future looks.

> *Note: If your child is really reluctant to draw pictures, you can ask them to describe the scene in detail to you and make notes instead. The aim of the exercise is to get as much detail as possible recorded – remember to answer the questions at the beginning of the exercise.*

My new future looks like this:

Complete this sentence: *When I have a dry bed in the morning, this is what I will see, hear and feel…*

. . . .

. . . .

. . . .

. . . .

STEP 2: MY NEW FUTURE – WHAT WILL HAPPEN NEXT?

Now take a few moments to encourage your child to think about what else will happen as a result of having a dry bed. Ask the following questions:

- As well as having a dry bed, what else will change in your life? Will it change the way you feel?
- And what about the other people around you? How will they feel? Imagine who else will be there first thing in the morning and the kind of things that they might say.
- Imagine yourself being successful and having a dry bed – will it mean you can start to do different things, like have sleepovers with friends? Will it mean you can go on holidays and school trips more easily? Will it mean no more wet sheets that have to be carted off to the washing machine and no more having to make up a fresh bed at night?
- What's the very best thing that will happen to you when you are dry at night?

What will you see?

What will you hear?

What will you feel?

Complete this sentence: *When I have a dry bed it will mean that...*

. . . .

. . . .

. . . .

. . . .

Ask your child to pick two examples and draw pictures below to show how much better things will look.

9

.

Day 2

Mind Over Body

Welcome to Day 2 of the programme – progress is being made.

As before, take a few moments to discuss and review the ideas that came up for you and your child in the previous activities. Talking will help reinforce ideas in your child's mind.

STEP 1: HOW MY BODY WORKS

It's important for your child to have a better understanding of how the body works and what it's going to be asked to do. Explain to your child that the mind and body are connected and they have a conversation with each other throughout the day.

Sometimes our bodies tell us what to do and sometimes we tell our bodies what to do.

Your body tells you:

- If you're too hot – *you might want to take your jumper off.*

- If you're too cold – *you'll feel like putting a jumper on.*

- If you're hungry – *your tummy will start to rumble.*

- If you're thirsty – *your mouth will feel dry.*

- If you're tired – *you'll start yawning.*

And then there are those other times when you tell your body to do things, for example:

- You tell it to run.
- You tell it to jump.
- You tell it to speak out loud.
- You tell it to pick up a pencil and write.

And telling your body to *hang on and walk to the bathroom to use the toilet* if you need to, is just one more of those things you'll be able to teach it to do.

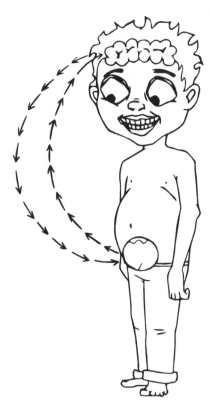

STEP 2: CONTROLLING MUSCLES

The bladder is a pouch or bag made of muscle that opens and closes as it tenses and relaxes.

Our bodies are full of muscles that can do this – we have them in our arms and legs, fingers and toes and we can tell them exactly what to do. We tell the muscles in our bodies to do things all the time.

Take a few moments, find a quiet space to sit or lie down with your child and discover what I mean as you play this game with your child.

Hands: Clench each fist (one at a time) for three seconds and then relax it for three seconds.

Arms: Bend each elbow so the wrist nearly touches the shoulder (one at a time) and hold for three seconds, then relax each arm for three seconds.

Legs: Point the toes and straighten the leg, pushing the knee down, so both the calf and thigh muscles tighten for three seconds, then relax this leg for three seconds. Repeat with the other leg.

Shoulders: Pull the shoulders up to the ears (or as close as they can get) and hold for three seconds, then relax for a further three seconds.

Eyes: Scrunch up the eyes so that they are tightly shut for three seconds. Then relax the eyes, but keep them shut for at least three more seconds.

You can ask your child to do other simple exercises too. For example:

- Jumping up and down on the spot.

- Standing still with arms outstretched, pretending to be a tree as they wave them from side to side.

- Get down on all fours and slowly crawl around the floor, growling like a lion.

Tell your child that each time they scrunch up their muscles or move their body around, they are telling it what to do.

Your child's response might be that they didn't say a word and that they didn't tell their body what to do. Point out that this happens 'silently' in their head – a bit like silent reading at school.

Our bodies are listening all the time, waiting for us to tell them what to do next. You are the boss of your body – you just hadn't realised it before.

And learning how to send commands to the muscles of the bladder is just one more of those things they can easily learn.

STEP 3: TELL YOUR BODY WHAT TO DO

An affirmation is a sentence or statement that you can say out loud or think to yourself repeatedly. These are really useful to cancel out negative thoughts and send a powerful message to the mind (and therefore the body) to start a new pattern of behaviour.

As your child is beginning to understand that they are the 'boss' of their bodies and, perhaps without having realised it before, they have control of all their actions, I'm going to suggest using the following sentences. Ask your child to repeat these each evening and every morning too.

> *I want to*.....keep my bed dry at night.
>
> *I can*............keep my bed dry at night.
>
> *I will*.......... keep my bed dry at night.
>
> *I do* ....keep my bed dry at night.

I love using this sequence of sentences – there's less resistance from the mind when you use words that build up to success gradually – so when you use the

> *I want to...*
>
> *I can...*
>
> *I will...*
>
> *I do (or I am)...*

sequence, it's easier to persuade your mind that this is something that can naturally happen. (For the last sentence, please use 'I do' or 'I am', whichever is grammatically most appropriate.)

You'll notice that I filled in the blank spaces with 'keep my bed dry at night'. You can use whichever words you feel are most appropriate, for example you might want to use phrases like these to complete your sentences:

> ... fall asleep easily.
>
> ... feel calm and relaxed at bedtime (or night-time).
>
> ... keep my bed dry tonight and each and every night.
>
> ... wake up quickly when I need to use the toilet.
>
> ... find my way to the bathroom easily.
>
> ... feel confident.

The more specific your words, the better. So, rather than 'keep my bed dry', add in the extra details of 'tonight' and then 'each and every night'.

Your child can also use these affirmations in other areas of their life too, for example:

> *I want to...* remember the correct answers for the school test tomorrow.
>
> *I want to...* run really fast in the race tomorrow.

Remind your child that when you go to a restaurant you always order what you *do* want to eat, rather than what you *don't*, e.g. *'spaghetti bolognese please'*, rather than, *'I don't want the burger, I don't want the chicken nuggets either or the fish fingers'*, in the hope that the waiting staff will guess what it is that you want to eat. That's not the best way to do things.

You have to be specific or you might find yourself with the wrong dish. And in just the same way, your mind and body are listening to what it is you are ordering off the 'menu of life'. Remember to order the right thing – *'I want to keep my bed dry'* rather than *'I want to stop wetting my bed'*.

You can finish off this exercise by writing your affirmations here or on a large piece of paper and sticking them on the bedroom wall.

. . . .

. . . .

. . . .

. . . .

. . . .

10

•

Day 3

Close That Gate

Yesterday, you and your child discovered how your mind and body work by talking to each other. And you also discovered how you can make those muscles tighten and then relax again, simply by thinking about it.

In just the same way, it's possible to control the bladder – opening it and closing it as and when needed. The muscles act like a 'gate' on the bladder.

Try this experiment with your child and you'll see what I mean.

Handy tip: Trying this in the bath may be the best place!

WATER BALLOON EXPERIMENT

1. Take an ordinary party balloon (a round one is best) and attach it to the end of a cold water tap.

2. Switch the tap on slowly and watch as the water begins to fill the balloon. Keep going until it's a bit bigger than a tennis ball. Switch the water off.

3. Now, very carefully take the balloon off the tap and squeeze the open end between your thumb and one of your fingers, to make sure the water can't come out.

4. Turn the balloon upside down over the sink. This is similar to how your bladder looks. Slowly, begin to relax your fingers slightly and allow some water to begin trickling out of the end. This is just how water comes out of your bladder when you go to the toilet.

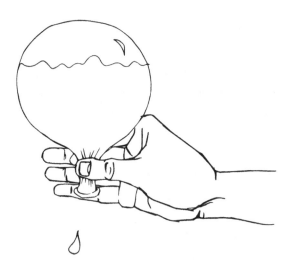

5. Now let's see if we can stop this flow. Squeeze your fingers tight once more and you'll discover that you can easily stop the water coming out.

6. Relax your fingers a little once more and let a bit more water out.

7. And then squeeze them tightly shut to stop the flow once more.

This is exactly how your muscles work – squeezing tight to hold urine in the bladder and relaxing to let it out – just like opening and closing a gate.

You and your child can practise this exercise again and again. Keeping this gate tightly closed is just what your child's body needs to learn to do at night to help them keep their bed dry.

TOILET EXERCISE

You can follow this exercise with some practice in the toilet. Ask your child to drink a large glass of water and wait for it to fill up their bladder. Then when they feel the urge to go to the toilet, ask them to practise using those muscles by stopping and starting the flow of urine. See how strong those muscles really are. Remind your child that they do a really good job of holding in their wee during the day when they're at school or out and about. The muscles keep the bladder firmly closed until it's convenient to go to the toilet. In just the same way, those muscles can do their job at night-time.

Note: Please ensure that your child knows they need to empty their bladder fully after this exercise. It's not advisable to hang on to urine after the urge to urinate has been experienced. This is a one-off exercise so they can locate their muscles and see how strong they are and not something I recommend doing on a regular basis.

GATE VISUALISATION

Now that we know how the muscles in our body open and close across the opening of the bladder just like a gate, we're going to take a closer look at your child's 'gate'. Everyone's 'gate' is different and I wonder what your child's will look like?

1. Settle yourselves down somewhere comfortable. Ask your child to close their eyes and just take a few moments to visualise the gate to their bladder. Pause for a few moments to give your child time to do this.

2. Encourage them to describe it clearly to you:
   - What colour is it?
   - How does it open?
   - Does it have a lock or bolt on it?
   - Is the lock tightly shut right now?

3. Ask your child to tell you what needs to be done to make sure this gate is firmly shut at night. (Allow your child's imagination to take over here – some children invent gatekeepers, or put extra big locks on the gate, others even have pets or animals keeping guard.)

Ensure your child's gate will not leak – many children visualise a gate that's similar to their own garden gate with wooden slats and this may not be suitable for holding back liquid because there are lots of gaps. Use the word 'door' if you feel this would be more appropriate.

Now ask your child to draw a picture of this gate:

My gate looks like this:

AFFIRMATIONS

Finish off today's exercise by repeating yesterday's affirmations out loud.

11
•
Day 4

Pump Up the Volume

Welcome to Day 4 – you're halfway through the programme now.

Take some time to review and chat about the exercises from the previous days. If you feel there is any confusion or lack of understanding, you'll be able to remind your child that each day they are getting closer and closer to achieving their goal – dry nights forever!

Note: From tomorrow your child will need to start listening to the hypnotic recording 'Dry Beds Now'. If you haven't done so already, please download it from my website now at www.stop-bed-wetting-in-7-days.com.

The recording is free of charge and getting it now means you'll have it to hand when you need it.

STEP 1: VOLUME CONTROL EXERCISE

Some nights it isn't going to be possible to wait until morning to visit the toilet – some nights your child may need to get up and go to the loo. We already know this.

But in the past, your child's mind and body haven't been communicating well enough to enable this to happen. Your child has remained in bed and you've dealt with the consequences in the morning.

During the day, your child gets lots of messages from their bladder. A little voice in their head says, *'Need to go to the toilet'*, and your child responds by walking to the bathroom and successfully dealing with the situation. Point this out to your child and ask them to pay specific attention to what receiving this message feels like over the next few days.

During the night, your child is asleep. So, when that little voice pipes up, *'Need to go to the toilet'*, it doesn't get heard.

There's a very simple solution to this. Let's turn the volume UP!

Take a few moments to run through this activity with your child. Begin by explaining to your child that they hear that little voice inside their head many times a day. It not only speaks up when your body needs to go to the loo, but it's the same voice that says:

> *'Hmm, I'm hungry, I fancy a biscuit.'*

> *'I'm feeling hot – I want to take my jumper off.'*

> *'I wonder what's on television.'*

And getting it to speak a little louder at night-time is just one of those things that can easily be done.

1. Ask your child to think of a favourite piece of music. This could be a song that they really like, the theme tune to a TV programme or even the 'Happy Birthday' song.

2. Ask them to tell you what it is and to just let themselves hear that music playing in their imagination, i.e. not out loud. Keep playing this music for a few moments.

3. Now it's time for a bit of fun. Get your child to play around with the volume by saying. 'I wonder if you can make it just a little bit quieter? And a little bit quieter still?' You can start to whisper these instructions, so your child will follow your lead. Pause here for a few moments to allow your child to do this.

4. And now you can turn the volume up by saying 'And how about making it louder? And a bit more? I wonder if you can make it so loud that it would wake the baby/frighten the dog (or similar)?' Use a louder and louder voice to do this, so again your child will follow your lead. Pause for a few moments to allow your child to do this. It's usual to see an intense look of concentration accompanied by a few giggles as they get the hang of this.

5. Take a few more moments to play around, turning the volume back down so it's nice and quiet and up, up, up so it's really loud once more.

STEP 2: THE VOLUME CONTROL

We don't know what your child's volume control looks like. Each one of us has a control that looks slightly different.

Point out to your child some of the different controls that can be found around the house, for example the light switch that flicks on and off, or maybe it's a dimmer that rotates around. Some switches are dials, others are levers and some have buttons like the controls for the television.

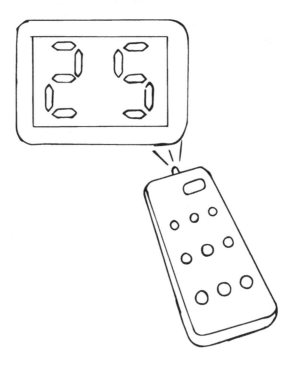

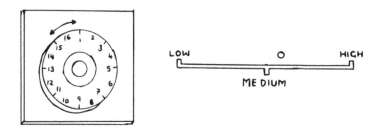

1. Ask your child to close their eyes for a few moments to take a really good look at the volume control that controls the sounds inside their mind.

2. What colour is it? How about the shape – is it round, square or long? Does it have a dial or a button? Or perhaps a slider? Or maybe it's digital and has a remote control?

3. How do they know which setting it's on – does it have numbers 1–10 or higher? Or does it say low–medium–high?

4. Ask your child to play around with the volume setting – can they turn it right down low? And then right up high, so it's very much louder?

5. Ask your child to notice how playing around with this control alters the volume of the little voice inside their head.

Ask your child to draw a picture of their very own special volume control here:

This is my volume control:

Now that we know what that all-important volume control looks like, your child will be able to easily programme it each night before going to sleep.

YOUR AUTOMATIC PILOT

We've all had situations where we've had to get up extra specially early in the morning – perhaps to go off on holiday and catch an early morning flight.

Have you ever set the alarm clock for some crazy time like 4 a.m., worried that you might oversleep but somehow miraculously found yourself automatically waking up five minutes before the alarm goes off?

It's a strange feeling, isn't it? People often wonder why that happens – in reality, not only do we set the alarm clock but we also programme our subconscious minds to wake us up as we're doing it. So, when we wake up early, we're literally operating on 'automatic pilot'.

In just the same way, your child can programme their very own 'autopilot' to wake themselves up when they receive that signal from their bladder.

ADJUSTING THE VOLUME

1. Ask your child to close their eyes and see in their imagination the volume control for their bladder – this may look a little different to the one that was controlling the music – check with your child and ask them to describe it once more.

2. What is the control set at? Is it set on high? Or is it set on low? Should it be adjusted?

3. Pause for a few moments here to allow your child to make whatever adjustments they feel are necessary to set this volume control on a loud enough setting to wake them up during the night, should they need to visit the toilet.

Every evening just before settling down for the night, your child will need to run through this activity and just check the control is set at the right level.

SAYING WHAT YOU WANT

Keeping in mind the importance of thinking and saying what it is we *do* want to happen, rather than what we *don't* want to happen, ask your child to spend a few moments each evening saying the following phrases out loud just before going to bed.

These phrases will be the equivalent of setting that alarm clock – your child's autopilot:

- *Message to my bladder:* Tonight as I sleep and dream, send a really loud message to let me know you're filling up.

- *Message to my volume control:* I'm turning the volume up really loud so I can hear my bladder telling me if I need the bathroom.

- *Message to my control gate:* Remember to keep the gate firmly shut until I'm awake and can get to the bathroom in time.

Just as you did with the affirmations, saying these phrases slowly, deliberately and out loud will send a flow of energy, almost like a crackle of electricity, down a particular neural pathway creating that vital link between mind and body. Be creative – invent some more commands that your child can send to their body.

Handy tip: Either you or your child can copy these sentences on to sticky notes and put them up on the wall next to the bed. Each evening, just before tucking down to sleep, your child will be able to say them out loud once more.

12

•

Day 5

Programming Your Sat Nav

Welcome to Day 5. Praise your child for having done really well to get this far. There are not too many days to go now. Remind them that in just a couple of days, they'll be enjoying the benefits of having those 'dry nights'.

As your programme progresses and the activities begin to build up, you may want to review yesterday's homework at a different time to introducing the new ones today. There is just one visualisation exercise to carry out today and your child will need to start listening to the audio recording, 'Dry Beds Now', which you can download free from my website at www.stop-bed-wetting-in-7-days.com. Have you downloaded your copy yet?

STEP 1: SAT NAV PROGRAMMING

Most of us wouldn't set off on a long journey without putting our destination into our satellite navigation systems or getting some directions from the Internet on our phones or computer. Only when we have a pretty good idea of where we're heading and how to get there, do we set off.

Expecting your child to get up in the middle of the night, in the dark and visit the bathroom in a semi-conscious state is a bit like playing 'blind man's buff' at a children's party. It's no wonder most kids opt to stay in bed and not venture out. So how can we give your child a map to navigate by?

Setting Up the Sat Nav

Begin by starting this activity during the daytime when there is some light and it is a little less daunting for your child. After the first couple of attempts, you can close the bedroom curtains to make it more realistic. It's really important to reinforce your child's perception of themselves as someone who can easily get up and walk to the bathroom at night, should they need to. The more this is 'rehearsed', the more likely your child is to be successful.

1. Ask your child to climb into bed and snuggle down under the covers, as if going to sleep at night.

2. Next, ask them to imagine that they've just received the message that the bladder needs to empty. Ask them to turn the volume up and really hear that voice inside their head.

3. Guide your child out of bed and walk slowly together along the route to the bathroom.

4. As you're walking along describe the route out loud, e.g. turn left, straight along for six steps, out of the door, into the hallway, eight steps past the cupboard and Mum and Dad's bedroom, a few more steps and into the bathroom. Describe the route exactly as you see it and write it down on a piece of paper.

5. Repeat this process several more times, until your child knows it off by heart and can say it out loud by themselves.

Making Sure the Sat Nav Is Fully Programmed

Having established the best route for your child to use at night-time, it's time to ensure that this becomes firmly imprinted on their mind by rehearsing it over and over again. This way, their personal 'sat nav' system is fully programmed.

Remember, if your child needs to go to the bathroom during the night, they will only be semi-conscious – this needs to be something they can do without thinking. If they are sleeping on an elevated bed such as a bunk, it may be wise to think about making a few changes during this programme so it is easier for them to get out of bed in the middle of the night.

1. Ask your child to lay down on the bed once more and this time close their eyes. Once again, ask them to imagine that they've just received the signal (i.e. heard that very loud voice) from their bladder and need to go to the toilet.

2. This time, they can picture themselves walking to the bathroom in their imagination. They won't need to do it 'for real', but your child will need to describe the route to the bathroom out loud a couple of times over. As you listen to this, check that their details are correct.

3. Now they'll be ready to just run through the scenario in their minds without saying anything at all. Repeat this several times over.

Remember, our bodies can't tell the difference between a real and an imagined event. This is a very clever way of 'rehearsing' the future, tricking your body into believing that you have done this before – making it all the easier to do it 'for real' when the time comes.

STEP 2: LISTENING TO THE AUDIO RECORDING

Have you downloaded your free audio recording from the website yet?

This audio recording called 'Dry Beds Now' lasts around 20 minutes. Your child will need to have a quiet place to listen to this. It's filled with positive messages that will reinforce all the work we've done so far.

It can be listened to once your child is in bed, instead of a bedtime story. However, as it's possible they will drift off to sleep while listening to it, I'd recommend giving them the opportunity to listen to it earlier in the day too. It's not necessary to be laying down with eyes closed – if your child is having a quiet moment playing with toys or games, for example, you can have the recording playing in the background.

Please DO NOT play it while you are driving in the car, unless your child is listening through headphones. It's very relaxing and will encourage you to close your eyes!

> *Note: If your child finds this audio recording a little too 'young' for them, it is possible to purchase a different one from my website called 'Stop Bedwetting Now', which is designed for older children and teenagers.*

Before your child goes to sleep tonight, I recommend running through this short list of activities.

Tonight's Bedtime Checklist

- Visualise gate on bladder and close it tight. ☐

- Set volume control on HIGH. ☐

- Speak 'autopilot phrases' out loud. ☐

- Programme sat nav. ☐

- Listen to audio recording. ☐

13

•

Day 6

Booking a Wake-Up Call

Welcome to Day 6 of this programme. Are you ready for the next stage? Do remember that I said it was possible to slow things down and repeat some of the previous activities if you feel your child would benefit from some extra time to assimilate all the information given so far.

It's always better to do *something* rather than nothing though, so it doesn't matter whether that's simply drawing another picture, running through a visualisation exercise, the affirmations and the commands, or just relaxing and listening to the audio recording – it's important do whatever you feel would be right for your child at this moment.

BOOKING A WAKE-UP CALL

In Chapter 5, I talked about how 'self-image' can play an important part in our ability to overcome problems and change habits. Many parents tell me that their child is a deep sleeper and nothing will wake them up – not even a traditional bedwetting alarm. Often this disturbs the entire household and not the child it was intended for.

I believe that rather than relying on an alarm on the 'outside' to wake your child, it would be better if they built one on the 'inside'.

Over time, your child will have gathered much evidence to support the notion that 'nothing will wake them' either through overhearing this being said about them or through direct experience.

Step 1

It's time to gather evidence to the contrary. Your child has the ability to wake themselves up at a particular time very easily. Think back to some of these occasions:

- Christmas or traditional festival
- birthday
- first day back at school
- holiday
- arrival of a new sibling or family pet
- return of a parent from a business trip
- school play
- exams

I'm sure you can think of many more. A mixture of excitement and anxiety the night before an event meant your child 'programmed' their mind to wake up at a particular time and, most likely, woke up five minutes before they were due to. We've all done this and most of us wondered how it happened.

Let's do some programming right now:

I'd like you to ask your child to remember all those occasions when, contrary to popular belief, they did wake up early, almost to order. Write these down, make a list and discuss it for around 15 minutes.

Now point out all the things that they would have done the night before. Perhaps:

- packing a suitcase
- hanging up Christmas stockings
- last-minute revision
- laying out special clothes

All these little things would have contributed to the 'programming' part of the wake-up process. Not only was your child performing these tasks but also making very clear pictures inside their mind of the forthcoming events. They went to sleep with these images milling around and, lo and behold, they woke up early. So we know it's possible.

Step 2

In the second part of today's activities, you're going to ask your child to create an alarm or something similar. To trigger off your child's creative processes, I sometimes refer to action movies such as *James Bond*. Quite often the final 15 minutes of that type of film involve a timer, clock or buzzer counting down two minutes before some kind of explosion or eruption occurs. This may inspire your child.

On the other hand, I've come across many children for whom the word 'alarm' can be quite upsetting – especially if they've used a bedwetting alarm in the past. And of course, alarms are often associated with emergency situations so it's not surprising. Choose your terminology carefully and ensure it suits your child.

They could choose a buzzer, a bell or even use music. Perhaps they would simply prefer to imagine a 'buddy' standing by the gate to their bladder and keep a watchful eye – as soon as their bladder reaches 98% full, it could be the buddy's job to sound the signal. This buddy could be their favourite superhero or footballer, best friend or family pet such as a dog barking. Let your child's imagination guide them – who do they feel confident about choosing? Who will be reliable, take the task seriously and help them to wake up on time?

1. Pick a quiet moment and ask your child to lay down on their bed and take a few moments to relax. They can do this exercise with their eyes open or closed – whichever suits them best.

2. Ask them to visualise the gate on their bladder once more – perhaps this is an ideal opportunity to make any adjustments or changes to it. Does it look as if it will leak? Should it be altered in any way?

3. Once this has been done, explain that it's time to put in an extra 'early warning system'. Ask your child to be creative here and design a system that feels right for them.

4. Some children choose to put glass panels on the side of their bladders so the buddy can see how quickly it's filling up. Others will create a sensor that can in some way detect this. And then it's important to create a button, lever or dial that will trigger off a sound.

5. Allow your child to experiment with sounds. Remember that volume control from the earlier exercise. Does your child wish to create speakers either side of the gate to really boom out the sound of the wake-up call?

6. And when does your child want the wake-up call to go off? When their bladder is full might just be too late. Would they prefer to set it for a couple of minutes beforehand to give them plenty of time to get out of bed and off to the bathroom? Would that be 80% or 90% full? Does there need to be a line or mark on the glass panel to indicate this? All these details need to be considered.

When your child is finished, offer them a large sheet of paper and some coloured pens. Ask them to draw the picture that they saw in their mind.

Some children create quite complicated alarm systems that can turn out to be quite confusing. While it's important for children to create this for themselves, I do feel it's fine to guide them a little, to get a clear picture in their minds of how the whole system will work.

Tonight's Bedtime Checklist

- Visualise gate on bladder and close it tight. ☐

- Set volume control on HIGH. ☐

- Affirmations and autopilot phrases. ☐

- Programme sat nav. ☐

- Check your wake-up call is set. ☐

- Listen to audio recording. ☐

14

•

Day 7

Overcoming Doubts

As you and your child reach the final day of preparation for your new life of 'dry beds forever', now is the time to take a few moments to check if there are any last-minute doubts, worries or niggles that could hold your child back. Tonight, you'll be repeating several of the activities.

Tomorrow you'll be leaving those protective pull-up pants or nappies behind forever. The time for collecting up every last one in the house and disposing of them for good is not very far away!

First of all, it's important to check that each and every 'part' of you and your child is happy with the decision to move forward in this way. It's common to feel in 'two minds' about certain things because two minds are exactly what we have – our conscious mind and our subconscious mind. It's easy to feel as if we know what we want to achieve on the outside, but sometimes our subconscious can almost sabotage our attempts.

How many of us adults want to lose weight, but on the other hand also really fancy that extra piece of chocolate cake? Have you ever wanted to get fit and go to the gym, but on the other hand really wanted to stay on the sofa and watch a movie?

The same goes for our children. Perhaps, on the one hand, they really want to spend time doing their school homework to get good marks, but on the other hand, they also want to spend time playing a video game or watching TV.

Success becomes much harder to achieve when there's an internal struggle going on. Take a few moments now to discuss any last-minute doubts or worries that both of you may be having.

Perhaps you're really looking forward to having dry nights forever with no more pull-ups, but on the other hand, you also want to ensure the bed sheets are dry. On the one hand, it would be nice to save lots of money from not having to buy protective pants or pull-ups, but on the other hand, will the money be spent on lots of extra washing of wet sheets?

Perhaps your child is looking forward to having sleepovers with their friends, but on the other hand, the safety and security of home where they can keep their pull-ups on is also appealing?

All these negative feelings serve a purpose – they are trying to protect you and your child and their intention is good. Even though it feels as if you are being pulled in two different directions, both sides only want the best for you. However, those feelings can have a sabotaging effect and hold you back from what you'd really like to achieve. Always keep in mind your ultimate goal – what would you really like to have happen? What is your dream?

ACHIEVING AGREEMENT

1. Take a few moments to identify any last minute worrying beliefs that you or your child may have. You may want to discuss these issues and write them down.

2. Once you and your child have done this, place your hands out in front of you with your palms facing up to the ceiling. Imagine the part that wants dry beds in your right hand and the other part, the bit that sometimes holds you back, in your left.

3. As you look at each hand in turn, ask the part what its positive intention is for you.

    So, for example, in the right hand you might have the part of you that really wants to get rid of pull-ups – and in the left hand you might have the part of you that worries about how you're going to cope without them.

On the one hand, your child might be really looking forward to their friend's sleepover party, but on the other hand, they might not want to go in case they have an accident.

On the one hand, your child knows it will be good to discuss this with family members or a teacher or friend to get extra support, but on the other hand, it's so embarrassing to talk about this problem.

On the one hand, your child knows they should drink more water during the day as it will be better for them, but on the other hand, they're worried they will need the toilet more often at school.

On the one hand, you know it will be good to follow this programme each evening, but on the other hand, you're not sure you'll have enough time.

Continue asking each part until it becomes increasingly obvious that they both want the same thing for you – namely, to keep you safe and happy with dry beds and success. The negative parts are not really try to sabotage your efforts, they're simply concerned and looking out for you.

4. Keep running through this process, even if it feels a little strange to begin with. Doing this will create changes in your confidence and self-belief.

5. Imagine a new 'super-part' emerging in the space between your hands. A 'super-part' that has the resources to keep both sides happy and still create success for you. This super-part knows and understands all the kinds of problems that we face, but it's clever and will find solutions for you.

   As you look down into this space, you may want to give it a colour – a special colour – a colour that feels right for you.

6. Now moving quickly, bring your hands together and allow those two separate parts to merge with the super-part and become one.

7. Raise your hands up to your chest and bring them in, allowing this new super-part to become fully absorbed and integrated as a new bit of you.

8. Close your eyes and enjoy this feeling of having every bit of your body in agreement about the kind of future you'll have.

As you practise this technique, you'll find all those feelings of internal conflict begin to simply disappear. You and your child both have a goal in mind – dry beds forever – and as all those parts line up in agreement, you'll find it easier to achieve just that.

Tonight's Bedtime Checklist

- Visualise gate on bladder and close it tight. ☐

- Set volume control on HIGH. ☐

- Affirmations and autopilot phrases. ☐

- Programme sat nav. ☐

- Check your wake-up call is set. ☐

- Listen to audio recording. ☐

15

•

Day 8 and Beyond

Well done! You've reached the end of the programme and the beginning of that new future.

Each day for the next week, it is important for your child to continue to listen to the audio recording that you've downloaded.

Additionally, there'll be that bedtime checklist of activities to run through.

NO MORE PROTECTIVE NIGHT-TIME PANTS

You have now reached the moment where you can throw out those nappies, pull-ups, alarms – whatever it was you were using at night, but remember it's still ok to protect the bed using absorbent mats or sheets.

Spend some time with your child and hunt through your cupboards, under the beds and even in the garage, to track down every last pull-up in the house. Bundle them all together in a plastic sack and throw them as far away as possible – get them out of the house! As your child's mind and body start to work closer together than ever before, you'll both discover that you no longer need them.

Really enjoy this moment together – this is an important step forward in your child's development and the more confident you can be as you do this, the more confident your child will feel.

I am often asked by clients, 'Should I keep a couple of pull-ups just in case?' As tempting as this might be, I would recommend that you don't. 'Just in case' or 'for emergencies' really means 'in case this doesn't work' and you'll be programming your mind to do just that – fail. Programme your mind for success and you'll succeed.

More importantly, getting rid of the pull-ups is sending a clear message to your child that you really expect them to succeed. Remember, we transmit messages through our body language and our actions, as well as our words.

Bedtime Checklist

- Repeat clenching muscles and balloon exercises as often as you like. ☐

- Visualise gate on bladder and close it tight. ☐

- Set volume control on HIGH. ☐

- Affirmations and autopilot phrases. ☐

- Programme sat nav. ☐

- Check your wake-up call is set. ☐

- Listen to audio recording. ☐

RECORDING SUCCESS

Keeping track of progress will spur your child on to even greater success. Tell your child that from now on they're going to have to remember to behave like a 'detective' – noticing small changes, collecting evidence and proof that they're moving closer and closer each day to their goal.

It's going to be important to keep a record of all successes, big and small, rather than simply keeping a record of dry nights or wet nights. There may be the occasional wet night and, if this does happen, your child's detecting powers will need to be even more special to find out the cause of the wet night.

Record any proof or evidence of successfully keeping to the system and leaving old habits and behaviours behind. This could be as simple as listening to the recording before bedtime and carrying out some of the visualisation exercises. Even the act of going to bed without wearing protective pants is a huge step forward and deserves to be recorded as success, as does helping to sort out the laundry if there is the odd wet night. So, even if an accident occurs, there is still progress that can be captured.

Some children report that, on occasions, although they didn't quite make it to the bathroom in time, they did wake up in time to be aware of wetting the bed. If in the past, your child would normally have slept right the way through, then they have made progress. It demonstrates that the messages are getting through, the system is working and they'll most probably be dry the next night.

Let's not forget, each small step forward, however small, is one step further forward in the process of having dry nights forever. The more 'success steps' you can record, the more you'll be helping your child to reach their overall goal.

You can record your child's progress in the 'success charts' provided here or you can download the 'Stop Bedwetting in Seven Days Diary' free from the website. Also, you can buy a separate notebook or diary for your child to use, should you prefer. As well as making a note of events on a daily basis, your child can also use this book to remind themselves of how different life will be in the future.

Encourage your child to be creative – maybe drawing more pictures or sticking in photos of friends they'd like to have sleepovers with, or even pictures of places they may go on overnight school trips.

Remember, thousands of children all around the world have used this system and successfully achieved those dry nights. Now, it's your child's turn to join them.

My Success Record

These were my achievements today:

Date: . . . .

. . . .

. . . .

. . . .

. . . .

. . . .

My Success Record

These were my achievements today:

Date: . . . .

. . . .

. . . .

. . . .

. . . .

. . . .

My Success Record

These were my achievements today:

Date: . . . .

. . . .

. . . .

. . . .

. . . .

. . . .

My Success Record

These were my achievements today:

Date: . . . .

. . . .

. . . .

. . . .

. . . .

. . . .

My Success Record

These were my achievements today:

Date: . . . .

. . . .

. . . .

. . . .

. . . .

. . . .

My Success Record

These were my achievements today:

Date: . . . .

. . . .

. . . .

. . . .

. . . .

. . . .

My Success Record

These were my achievements today:

Date: . . . .

. . . .

. . . .

. . . .

. . . .

. . . .

COOLING-OFF PERIOD

Once your child has been achieving dry nights for a few weeks, you can begin winding the activities down. I suggest that the audio recording is listened to just once or twice a week.

You can also review some of the exercises a couple of times during the week. It's very likely that your child will have got into a routine and will automatically repeat most of the exercises, without needing a reminder.

If your child continues to be dry, you'll be able to reduce to just once a week and see how things go.

CELEBRATING SUCCESS

Having successfully worked your way through this programme, you and your child will be able to look forward to that new future with 'dry beds forever'.

And if you find yourselves struggling, don't give up – there is always a solution to every problem. Read through the 'Frequently asked questions' at the end of this book for further help or visit the website for details of other resources that will also help.

This is not magic, but you might be surprised to discover that it might *seem* like magic!

Enjoy those sleepovers!

Alicia

16

•

Frequently Asked
Questions

Here are some of the most common questions I get asked by parents who ask me to help their children with bedwetting problems.

At what age do children usually become dry at night?
There's a complex coordination that needs to develop between nerves and muscles in order to control the bladder and this has usually taken place by the age of 5, but some children take a little longer. If your child has reached their 6th birthday and still regularly wets the bed, it's a good idea to consider this system to help them become dry.

How old does my child have to be to use this system?
Your child will need to be old enough to understand the problem and how they have a part to play in getting themselves dry and this will vary from child to child. All the techniques described in this book are suitable for use with young children and I have worked in similar ways with children as young as 4 years.

My child is not only wet at night but also has accidents during the day. He gets distracted and leaves it too late to visit the toilet resulting in wet patches on his trousers. Can this system help?
While this programme is not specifically designed to help with daytime accidents, many parents do find that working through the exercises does help to build up the child's self-awareness and as a result daytime wetness becomes a thing of the past. Many children fix their

daytime habits before their night-time ones, so applaud their progress and point it out to them, even if they haven't achieved dry nights yet. They are on the right track.

What happens if we miss doing the activities on one of the days?

Continue to work through the system on the next available day. Ensure your child can remember the previous activities well enough before moving on to the next one. Don't attempt to 'catch up' by doing two days' activities in one go and remember to alter any dates you may have marked in the calendar. However, once your child starts to listen to the audio recording, it's best not to miss a day for at least one week.

I can't eliminate all pull-up pants from the house as my child's 3-year-old sister is still wearing them at night. Is this a problem?

It's worth finding a new place to store younger siblings' protective night pants, perhaps even providing a new box or container for them to clearly indicate who they belong to. If they share a bedroom do store them as far away as possible.

My child has been dry for six nights but wet on the seventh. It was the same story the following week. Should I be thinking about doing something differently?

No. Your child has had 12 dry nights out of 14. That's fantastic progress! You've clearly being doing everything right and there's no need to think about changing anything. Remember to focus on your child's successes rather than any accidents that may occur along the way.

My child is really scared of the dark and I think this is the reason why he won't get up to go to the bathroom at night. What should I do?

If your child is suffering from anxiety for whatever reason – a fear of the dark or nightmares, exam stress or school pressures – then stress chemicals like cortisol and adrenaline will flood the brain and make it harder for your child's mind to acquire this new way of thinking. It's common to see this happen to contestants on TV quiz shows – their nervousness makes their minds go blank and they struggle to come up with a correct answer. If you feel your child is suffering from anxiety issues, don't despair or abandon the idea of solving their bedwetting problem. I have written other books that will help deal with the anxiety and you can read more about these on my website. Try to tackle this problem in the initial instance.

I can't get my child to sit still and listen to what I'm trying to explain to them. They fidget and then sometimes refuse to draw the pictures.

I'm sure most parents (me included) have experienced the feelings of frustration that come with helping a child with maths homework. Why is it that they don't want to listen to Mum or Dad but will quite happily listen to a maths tutor? It's so annoying! You may find following this bedwetting programme is a struggle if you already have a long history of trying to get your child dry at night. You will both have become annoyed with each other at times and your child may not be receptive to the idea of trying something new. Remember, children want their parents' approval more than anything and if your child feels that they're going to make a fool of themselves and have embarrassing accidents in front of you, then it's understandable that they may not be receptive to the idea of doing this with you.

Don't despair – I have recorded an online video programme of my system for precisely this reason. Rather than listening to you explain the system, your child can view a series of short video clips on their laptop or tablet and watch me running through the homework exercises. It's similar to coming in to my Harley Street practice and having a personal face-to-face session. As we all know, kids love watching screens, so you might find it doesn't take too much to encourage them to do this.

Alternatively, think about handing over to a 'buddy' – another family member, an auntie or uncle perhaps, or a family friend that your child looks up to.

I can't seem to get my child to follow one of the visualisation exercises – is this going to be a problem?
The more exercises your child can take part in, the better. However, it's not essential to follow each one in order to

have this process work. It's important for your child to have an understanding of how the mind and body work closely together and it's also important for your child to listen to the audio recording for several days. Thereafter, there is a degree of flexibility in the system. While I believe it's best to work through all the activities, I have had children who have become completely dry by just listening to my audio recording and doing no more.

Is listening to the audio recording an essential part of this programme? I feel my child is getting fed up of listening to it.
Different things work for different children and not everyone will get along with a listening activity and may prefer to do some drawing or writing instead. However, personally I would recommend it. Could you make it easier for your child by playing it in the background as they do other activities such as play with a puzzle on the floor? Would listening to it through a headset while travelling to school in the car be a more appealing way of doing it?

Other recordings are available from my website. For example, 'Stop Bedwetting Now' is designed for children up to teenage years and 'A Magic Day Out' is a general confidence-boosting story for 5–12-year-olds. I am adding to the list of recordings all the time, so do remember to check out the online shop for new titles.

My child has had some success but now seems to be getting despondent and angry. What can I do?

Hang on in there and don't be tempted to go back to old habits of wearing night-time protection pants or lifting. It's important to keep moving forwards and remembering that this is a really important life skill that your child needs to acquire. Following this programme means you're making life better for them, not worse – it may just take a bit of time for them to realise that.

You can read about how to help your child become more resilient and bounce back from failures in my other books (see the 'Also by Alicia Eaton' section at the end of this book).

My child has been dry for several months now but each time we visit the grandparents, he wets the bed. It's so embarrassing – how can I get him to stop? I know he's happy with the visits and I've checked his bedroom is cosy and he's not scared by anything there. What do you suggest?

This may not be purely coincidental and I would recommend taking a close look at what your child has to eat and drink while staying there. It could be triggered off by sugar-free squashes, fizzy drinks, milk, eating too much fruit or wheat. It's worth writing everything down and this should give you some clues as to why this could be happening.

My son has been really successful – six dry nights in a row. But now he's had three wet nights and is getting disheartened. How can I explain to him that this is normal?
It's a good idea to remind him that this is not the first time in his life that he's had to practise something before getting good at it (give him examples).

When children first learn how to swim, the teacher tells them what to do and how to move their arms and legs. To begin with, they have to 'think' about what they're doing and concentrate quite hard. This is the conscious mind working.

And then, as time goes by they get the hang of it and before they know it they can swim and chat to their friends at the same time. Their behaviour is now imprinted on their subconscious minds. And how good does that feel?

So, things are going well and then one day they go to their usual swimming class and for some reason, it's a struggle. Things just don't go as well as they usually do – it's an 'off' day. Those are the sort of days when mums and dads will be saying, 'I don't know what his problem is... last week he could do backstroke perfectly and now he's all over the place!' Does this sound familiar?

It's the same for any kind of new behaviour that our bodies are trying to learn – sometimes we have 'off' days. But that's all they are – just 'off' days. Reassure your child that he's doing well and continue to find 'evidence' that will support the notion that things are changing for the better.

Notes

About the Author

Originally a Montessori Teacher, Alicia Eaton ran her own school for five years and followed this up with further training and studies at the Anna Freud Centre in London. She then went on to train as a psychotherapist and clinical hypnotherapist as well as undertaking numerous trainings in neuro-linguistic programming (NLP). She also assisted Paul McKenna with his seminars for over seven years. A qualified Trainer of NLP, Alicia regularly speaks and runs workshops on a variety of topics, including parenting and emotional well-being.

Since 2004, she's run a successful practice in London's Harley Street helping both adults and children change unwanted habits and behaviours. Over the years, she has continued to add to her skills by training in mindfulness at the Oxford Mindfulness Centre and also as a practitioner of the latest psycho-sensory therapies such as Thought Field Therapy (TFT) and Havening.

Her work is regularly featured in the media and she's also the author of *Fix Your Life with NLP* (Simon & Schuster, 2012), *Words That Work: How to Get Kids to Do Almost Anything* (Matador, 2015) and *First Aid for Your Child's Mind* (Practical Inspiration, 2019).

Also By Alicia Eaton

First Aid For Your Child's Mind (2019)

Words That Work: How to Get Kids to Do Almost Anything (2015)

Fix Your Life with NLP: A First Aid Kit for the Mind (2012)

AUDIO DOWNLOADS FOR ADULTS AND CHILDREN

- Relax Now

- Boost Your Confidence

- Sleep Soundly

- Weight Off Your Mind

- Hypnotic Gastric Band

- Smoke Free

- Garden of Your Life

- Exam Success

- Dry Beds Now (Age 5–10)

- Stop Bedwetting Now (Age 8–Teens)

- A Magic Day Out

- The Sleepyhead Garden

- Fussy Eating No More

- Stop Thumbsucking Now

Made in the USA
Coppell, TX
01 October 2022

83899337R00128